Adamnani Vita S. Columbae

Prophecies, Miracles and Visions of St. Columba (Columcille)

First Abbot of Iona, AD. 563-597

By Saint Adamnan

Translated by Henry Frowde

PANTIANOS
CLASSICS

Published by Pantianos Classics

ISBN-13: 978-1-78987-534-8

First published in 1895

Contents

The Second Book, of Miracles of Power 46

Here Beginneth the Third Book, of Angelic Visitations 79

Note

IN the present translation, accuracy has been made a first considera-
tion, and hence the style and constructions of the original have often been
imitated where the words might have been put into better English. A few
explanatory notes and glosses have been added in the text.   For further
information the reader is referred to the Latin edition, with notes and
introduction, recently published by the Clarendon Press.

J. T. F.

Bishop Hatfield's Hall, Durham,
      May, 1895.

In The Name of Jesus Christ, Here Beginneth the Preface

FORASMUCH as I wish to comply with the importunities of the brethren, and am about to write, with Christ's help, the life of our blessed patron, I will first take care to remind my readers that they should give credence to the ascertained facts here related, and think of the matter rather than the words, which, as I myself consider, seem to be unpolished and rude, and should remember that the kingdom of God standeth not in abundance of speech, but in excellency of faith; and not despise the rehearsal of events profitable to us, and that happened not without the help of God, on account of some obscure names of persons, or tribes, or places in the barbarous Scotic (Irish) tongue, which are becoming, as I think, of small account among the various other languages of foreign nations. Moreover, we thought that the reader should be put in mind of this also, that we have omitted many things concerning this man of blessed memory for the sake of brevity, even things worthy of remembrance, and have recorded as it were just a few events out of many, lest we should weary our readers. And this, as I think, every one who reads these memoirs will perhaps note, that in comparison with these few which we are now taking in hand briefly to write down, the common report of the same blessed man which is noised abroad has scattered among the nations only the least of his most mighty deeds. Hence, after this first little preface, I will, by God's help, in the beginning of my second, first of all give some intimation concerning our abbot's name.

In The Name of Jesus Christ, the Second Preface

HE was a man of venerable life and blessed memory, a father and founder of monasteries, and his name was the same as that of Jonah the prophet, for, although different in sound in the three different languages, this word, which in Hebrew is pronounced as *Iona,* but which Greek utters as *Peristera,* is also in the Latin tongue translated *Columba.* Such and so great a name is believed to have been given to the man of God not without a Divine providence. For also according to the faith of the Gospels, the Holy Ghost is shown to have descended upon the Only-begotten of the Eternal Father in the form of that little bird which is called *columba* (dove); whence for the most part in the Holy Scriptures the dove is distinguished as mystically signifying the Holy Spirit. Accordingly the Saviour also in His Gospel taught His disciples to preserve the simplicity of doves implanted in a pure heart, for the dove is a simple and innocent bird. It was right therefore that a simple and innocent man, who by his dove-like disposition made a dwelling-place within himself for the Holy Spirit, should be called by this name, to which name not unfitly corresponds that which is written in the Proverbs, 'Better is a good name than great riches.' Not undeservedly, then, was this our abbot, being already adorned by the gift of God, endowed with this his proper name. Not only from the days of his infancy, but even while many a rolling year had yet to move before the day of his birth, he was, as if a child of promise, named in a wonderful prophecy, the Holy Spirit revealing it to a certain soldier of Christ. For a British stranger, a holy man, a disciple of the holy bishop Patrick, Mochta by name, so prophesied concerning our patron, as we now have it handed down to us from men of old who knew it as an ascertained fact. 'In the last ages of the world,' he says, 'a son is to be born, whose name Columba shall be spread abroad, known through all the regions of the isles of the ocean, and he shall brightly shine upon the last ages of the world. The grounds of the two monasteries of him and of myself will be separated by the space of one little fence; very dear to God shall the man be, and of great merit in His sight.'

In describing the life and character of this our Columba, I will in the first place, so far as I can, closely compress it in a short discourse, and at the same time set before the eyes of the reader his holy conversation. But I will also briefly mention, to be as it were eagerly tasted beforehand by my readers, certain of his miracles, which however will be more fully unfolded below, distributed through three books. The first of these will contain Prophetic revelations; the second, Divine powers exercised through him; the third, Angelic apparitions, and certain manifestations of celestial brightness upon the man of God. Let no one then regard me as saying anything untrue concerning this man, renowned as he was, or as one who would write doubtful or uncertain things; but be it known that I shall narrate those things which have been handed down in the consistent record of our ancestors and of faithful men who 'knew, and that I shall write without any ambiguity; and this either from what we have been able to find recorded in the pages of those who have gone before us, or from what we have learned on diligent inquiry, by hearing it from certain faithful ancients who told us without any hesitation.

St. Columba, then, was born of noble parentage; his father was Fedilmith son of Fergus, his mother Aethne by name, whose father can be called in Latin Filius Navis (son of Nave), but in the Scotic (Irish) tongue Mac Nave. In the second year after the battle of Cooladrummon, and the forty-second of his age, being desirous to make a journey for Christ from Ireland into Britain, he sailed forth. And he, who from his boyhood had been devoted to the service of Christ and the study of wisdom, preserving, by the gift of God, soundness of body and purity of soul, showed that though placed upon earth he was fitted for the heavenly life. For he had as it were the face of an angel, he was polished in speech, holy in work, the best of men in disposition, great in counsel, living for thirty-four years an island soldier (*i.e.* of Christ). Not even the space of a single hour could pass by without his devoting himself to prayer, or reading, or writing, or even to some manual labour. Day and night he was so engaged, without any intermission, in unwearied exercises of fasts and vigils, that the particular burden of any one labour might seem to be beyond human possibility. And meanwhile he was dear to all, ever showing a cheerful, holy face, and was gladdened in his inmost heart by the joy of the Holy Spirit.

Here Begins the Text of the First Book, of Prophetic Revelations

Chapter One - A Brief Narrative of Miracles of Power

SUCH evidences of his powers as the venerable man gave are now, in the beginning of this little book, to be briefly set forth, according to our promise given above (preface).

For in the Name of the Lord Jesus Christ, by virtue of his prayers, he healed persons suffering from attacks of various diseases; and by God's help he himself, single-handed, drove out malignant and innumerable hosts of demons warring against himself, seen by bodily eyes, and beginning to bring in deadly diseases upon his monastic society, but expelled from this our primatial island. By Christ's help he restrained the furious rage of beasts, partly by striking them dead, partly by brave repulse. Again, the swellings of the waves, sometimes rising all together mountains high in a mighty tempest, were soon quieted and brought low at his prayer, and his ship, in which he chanced to be sailing at that time, was brought to the desired haven in a great calm. When staying for some days in the territory of the Picts, on his return thence he ran up his sail against a contrary wind to confound the Druids, and so his ship, sailing out in a rapid course, made as swift a voyage as if he had had a fair wind. At other times, again, winds that were contrary for sailors were turned into favourable breezes at his prayer. In the same territory that has been mentioned above he took from a river a white stone, which he blessed to be of service for some cures, which stone, contrary to nature, on being dropped into water, swam on the surface as if it had been an apple. This Divine miracle was wrought in the presence of King Brude and his retinue. In the same province also he raised the dead son of a certain countryman that believed, and restored him alive and well to his father and mother, which is a still greater miracle. At another time, the same blessed man while a young deacon was residing in Ireland with Finbarr a holy bishop, and when the wine necessary for the all-holy mysteries fell short, he turned pure water into true wine by the power of prayer. But also a great light of heavenly brightness was occasionally seen by some of the brethren to be shed upon him, at different and separate times, both in the darkness of night and in the light of day. He merited also frequently to enjoy the delightful, most sweet, and luminous visits of holy angels. Often did he see the souls of certain righteous men borne by angels to the highest heavens, the Holy Spirit unveiling it to him. But also he many a time beheld other souls of evil men borne by demons to the infernal regions. He frequently foretold the future recompense of many while yet living in mortal flesh, the joys of some, the woes of others. In the terrific crashings of battles he obtained this from God by the powers of his prayers, namely, that some kings should be conquered, while other rulers should come off conquerors. And not only while yet his portion was in this present life, but even after his departure from the flesh, to him, as if to some victorious and most brave champion, was such a privilege as this vouchsafed by God, who does honour to all holy men. Of such honour conferred from heaven by the Almighty upon the honourable man, we will just give one example, which was manifested to Oswald the Saxon king the day before he engaged in battle with that most valiant of men, Cadwalla king of the Britons. For when the same King Oswald was encamped in preparation for battle, one day while sleeping on the pillow in his tent, he sees St. Columba in a vision, beaming with angelic beauty, and his lofty stature seeming to touch the clouds with the top of his head. Which blessed man, indeed, revealing his own name to the king, and standing in the middle of the encampment, covered the same, except one little distant point, with his shining raiment, and uttered these inspiring words, the same, namely, which the Lord spake to Joshua the son of Nun before his passing over Jordan after the death of Moses, saying, 'Be strong, and play the man; lo! I will be with thee,' &c. St. Columba accordingly, speaking these words to the king in the vision, adds:; This very night, go forth from the camp to the battle; for this time the Lord hath granted to me that thine enemies shall be put to flight, and thine adversary Cadwalla shall, be delivered into thine hands; and after the battle thou shalt return victorious, and shalt reign in felicity.' The king, being roused after these words, relates this vision to his assembled thanes; all are encouraged by it, the whole folk promise to believe and receive baptism after their return from the battle, for up to that time all that Saxon land (England) had been wrapped in the darkness of heathendom and ignorance, except King Oswald himself, with twelve men, who were baptized with him during his exile among the Scots (Irish). What more need I say? That very night King Oswald, as he had been instructed in the vision, goes forth from the camp to the battle, with a much smaller army, against many thousands, gains from the Lord a happy and easy victory, as it had been promised to him; and then, King Cadwalla being slain, and he himself returned victorious from the war, he is afterwards ordained by God as the Bretwalda (over-king) of all Britain. My predecessor, our abbot Failbhe, unhesitatingly related this narrative to me, Adamnan, and he declared that he had heard it from the mouth of King Oswald himself, as he related the same vision to the abbot Seghine. But this also seems to be a thing not to be passed by, that by means of certain songs in praise of the same blessed man, in the Scotic (Irish) tongue, and the commemoration of his name, some persons, although wicked and blood-thirsty men of lewd conversation, in that very night in which they had sung the same songs, were delivered from the hands of their enemies who had beset the house of the same singers. For they slipped out safe and sound between flames and swords and lances, while a few of their number, who, as if lightly esteeming the commemorations of the holy man, would not sing his praises, were the only ones that perished in that attack of their enemies. Witnesses to this miracle could be produced, not two or three, according to the law, but even a hundred, and more than that. And not only in one place or at one time is this same thing proved to have happened, but also at divers places and times in Scotia (Ireland) and in Britain has it been found without any doubt that the same has been done, still in a similar way and for a like cause, namely, that of deliverance. These things we have undoubtedly learned from men of experience of every district wherever the same thing has happened by a like miracle.

But, to return to the point in hand, among those miracles which the same man of the Lord, while living in mortal flesh, wrought by the gift of God, was this, that from the years of his youth he began also to be mighty in the spirit of prophecy, to predict things to come, to declare things at a distance to persons present, because although absent in the body, yet present in the spirit, he could discern things done afar off; for, according to the saying of Paul, 'He who cleaveth unto the Lord is one spirit.' Whence it was that the same man of the Lord, St. Columba, as he himself did not deny to some few brethren who sometimes inquired concerning this matter, in some contemplations of Divine grace he beheld even the whole world as if gathered together in one ray of the sun, gazing on it as manifested before him, while his inmost soul was enlarged in a wonderful manner.

We have here given this narrative of the virtues of the holy man, in order that he who reads more eagerly may, in the things which we have briefly written out, have as it were a foretaste of certain more delightful feasts that are yet to come; things which, with the Lord's help, shall be more fully recounted in the three following books. It seems to me not unfitting that I should now relate, albeit not in their proper sequence, the blessed man's prophecies which he delivered concerning certain holy and illustrious men at various times.

Chapter Two - Of St. Fintan the Abbot, Son of Tailchan

ST. FINTAN, afterwards reckoned throughout all the churches of the Scots (Irish) as a man of very high repute, preserving from boyhood, by God's help, purity of flesh and spirit, and devoted to the pursuit of Divine wisdom, had this purpose in his heart while yet passing through his youthful years, that he would take his leave of Ireland, and make a journey to visit our St. Columba. Burning with that same desire, he goes to a certain old man who was his friend, a most wise and venerable clerk in his own country, who in Scotic (Irish) was called Columb Crag, that from him, as from a judicious person, he might hear some sound advice. And when he opened out to him his thoughts of this kind, he received from him this answer: 'Who can hinder thy desire to sail across to St. Columba, devout and inspired by God as I believe it to be?' The same hour arrive by chance two monks of St. Columba, and they, being asked about their travels, say, 'We have lately rowed over from Britain, and to-day have come from Calgach's oak-wood' (Deny). 'Is your holy father Columba well?' asks Columb Crag. And they, with many tears and great sorrow, said, 'Our patron is indeed well, for not many days ago he departed to Christ.' On hearing this, Fintan and Columb and all who were within that place wept bitterly, prostrated with their faces to the earth. Fintan presently inquires, asking, 'Whom has he left after him as a successor?' 'Baithene,' they say, 'his foster son.' And as all cry, 'It is meet and right,' Columb says to Fintan, 'What wilt thou do now, Fintan?' Who answers and says, 'If the Lord will permit, I will sail forth to Baithene, that holy and wise man, and, if he will take me, I will have him as my abbot.' And thereupon, having kissed the above-mentioned Columb, and saying farewell to him, he prepares for sailing, and, sailing over without any, even the least, delay, arrives at the Iouan island (Iona). Now his name was not up to that time known in these parts. And hence it was that, being hospitably received in the first instance as some stranger unknown, on another day he sends a messenger to Baithene, being desirous to speak with him face to face. Who, affable as he was, and popular with strangers, bids that he be brought in to him; and he at once on entering, in the first place, as was right, prostrated himself on the ground on bended knees, but being bidden by the elder Saint, he rises, and, sitting down, is questioned by Baithene, who is not yet aware, concerning his nation and province, his name and manner of life, and his reason for undertaking the trouble of the voyage. And he, being thus questioned, tells all things in their order, and humbly begs to be admitted. And then the elder Saint, on hearing these things from his guest, and at the same time knowing him to be the man of whom St. Columba had prophesied some time before, says, 'I ought indeed to give thanks to my God upon thy arrival, my son; but know this without a doubt that thou wilt not be a monk of ours.' The guest, sadly distressed at hearing this, says, 'Perhaps I am so unworthy as not to deserve to become thy monk.' The elder thereupon replies, 'I did not say, as thou sayest, that thou wast unworthy; but although I would rather retain thee with me, yet I cannot violate the command of my holy predecessor Columba, through whom the Holy Spirit prophesied of thee. For thus he spake one day to me alone and apart, and in prophetic utterance, saying, among other things, "O Baithene, thou shouldest hearken very attentively to these my words, for immediately after my passing away, long waited for and greatly desired, from this world unto Christ, a certain brother from Scotia (Ireland) who at this time, well regulating his youthful age by a holy life, is well trained in sacred studies; his name is Fintan, of the tribe Mocumoie, and his father's name is Tailchan; he, coming to thee, I say, will humbly beg that thou wilt receive him and number him among the rest of thy monks. But this, namely, that he should himself become the monk of any abbot, has not been predestined for

18

him in the foreknowledge of God, but he has long ago been chosen of God as an abbot* of monks, and a leader of souls to the kingdom of heaven. Do not therefore retain this said man with thee in these our islands, lest thou shouldest seem also to fight against the will of God; but tell him these words, and send him back in peace to Scotia (Ireland), to establish a monastery in the parts of Leinster near to the sea, and there feed the flock of Christ's sheep, and lead souls innumerable to the heavenly country.'" On hearing these words the younger Saint gives thanks to Christ with many tears, saying, 'According to the prophetic and marvellous foreknowledge of St. Columba be it unto me.' And in those days, obeying the words of the Saints, and receiving a blessing from Baithene, he sails over in peace to Scotia (Ireland).

I learned these things as undoubted facts from a certain religious and aged presbyter, a soldier of Christ, Oisseneus by name, son of Eman, of the clan Mocu Neth Corb, who narrated them to me, and bore witness that he had himself heard the above-mentioned words from the mouth of the same St. Fintan son of Tailchan, whose monk he had been.

Chapter Three - A Prophecy of St. Columba Concerning Ernene Son of Crasene

AT another time the blessed man, while staying some months in the central part of Ireland, founding by Divine favour his monastery, which is called in Scotic (Irish) Dairmag (Durrow), thought it well to visit the brethren who were dwelling together in St. Kiaran's monastery at Clonmacnoise. And on hearing of his arrival, every one from the fields about the monastery, together with those who were found gathered together within it, following with all eagerness their abbot Alither, set off with one consent, going outside the enclosure of the monastery, to meet St. Columba, as an angel of the Lord. And they humbly bowed with their faces to the earth as they saw him, and with all reverence they kissed him, and raising their voices in hymns and praises, they conduct him through with all honour to the church. And, tying together a canopy (or barrier) of poles, they had it borne by four men walking in pairs, around the Saint as he walked, lest, mark you, a man of St. Columba's age should be thronged by the crowding together of such a multitude of the brethren. And in that same hour a certain servant-boy, much cast down in countenance and meanly clad, and not yet approved by his elders, came behind, hiding himself as much as he could, that he might touch even the fringe of that cloak which the blessed man wore, secretly, and if possible without his knowing or perceiving it. But yet this was not hidden from the Saint, for that which with his bodily eyes he could not see done behind him he perceived by spiritual vision. And so he suddenly stops, stretches out his hand behind him, catches the boy by the neck, and, drawing him forth, sets him in front of him, while all those who are standing around say, 'Send him away! Send him away! Why dost thou detain this wretched and troublesome boy?'

But the Saint, on the other hand, utters these prophetic words from his pure heart: 'Suffer it to be so now, brethren; suffer it to be so now.' But to the boy, who is trembling all over, he says, 'O my son, open thy mouth, and put out thy tongue.' Then the boy at his bidding, and with much trembling, opened his mouth and put out his tongue, and the Saint, stretching forth his holy hand, earnestly blesses it, and thus prophetically speaks, saying, 'Although this boy may now appear to you as one to be despised and of very low estate, yet let no one despise him on that account. For from this hour not only will he not displease you, but he will greatly please you, and in good conduct and the virtues of the soul he will by degrees advance from day to day; wisdom also and prudence shall from this day be increased in him more and more, and great is his future career in this your congregation; his tongue also shall be endued by God with wholesome doctrine and eloquence.' This was Ernene son of Crasene, afterwards famous and of the greatest note among all the churches of Scotia (Ireland).

And all these words above written, prophecies concerning himself, he narrated to the abbot Seghine, while my predecessor Failbhe, who himself also was there present with Seghine, was attentively listening, and from whose account I myself have come to know these same things which I have related. But there are many other things which the Saint prophesied in those days while he was lodged in the monastery of Clonmacnoise, the Holy Spirit revealing them unto him; as, for instance, about that disagreement which arose among the churches of Scotia (Ireland) about the different observance of the Paschal feast; and about certain visits of angels made to him, by which angels certain places within the enclosures of the same monastery were at that time frequented.

Chapter Four - Of the Arrival of St. Cainnech the Abbot, of Which St. Columba Made a Prophetic Announcement

AT another time, in the Iouan island (Iona), on a day of crashing tempest and terrible lifting up of the waves, the Saint, as he sat in his house, directed the brethren, saying. 'Prepare quickly a lodging, and draw water for washing the feet of guests.' And a certain brother of their number thereupon said, 'Who can safely sail across the Sound, narrow though it be, on a day like this, so fearfully windy as it is, and dangerous beyond measure?' On hearing which the Saint thus speaks: 'To a certain man, holy and elect, who will come to us before evening, the Almighty hath granted a calm, even in this storm.' And lo! the same day arrived a ship that had been some time expected by the brethren, with St. Cainnech on board, according to the prophecy of the Saint. The Saint with the brethren drew nigh to meet him, and he was received with distinction and hospitality. But those sailors who had been on board with Cainnech, being asked by the brethren what sort of a voyage they had

had, replied exactly as St. Columba had before said of the storm and the calm, wonderfully separated, God granting it, in the same sea, and at the same time; and they stated that they had not felt anything of the storm, though they had seen it from a distance.

Chapter Five - Of Peril by the Sea to the Holy Bishop Colman Mocusailni, Near the Island Called Rechru (Rathlin)

ON another day also, St. Columba, while residing at his mother church, suddenly smiling, broke out into these words, saying, 'Columban son of Beogna has just set out to sail over to us, and is even now in great danger in the surging waves of Brecan's whirlpool, and is sitting in the prow, lifting up both his hands towards heaven; he is also blessing that tempestuous and so dreadful a sea, yet the Lord is thus frightening him, not that he is to be overwhelmed in the waves by the wrecking of the ship in which he is sitting, but rather that he may be roused to pray more earnestly, that by God's help he may come through to us after the danger is past.'

Chapter Six - Of Cormac

AT another time also, St. Columba thus prophesied of Cormac Ua Liathain, a holy man undoubtedly, one who not less than three times with much trouble sought a desert island in the ocean, but without finding one, saying, 'To-day again is Cormac, desiring to find a desert island, beginning to sail out from that district which is situated beyond the river Moy, and is called Erris of the Damnonii; yet he will not even this time find what he seeks, and for no other fault than that he has taken with him on his voyage a monk of a certain religious abbot without first obtaining his leave, a deserter indeed, who ought not by right to accompany him.'

Chapter Seven - Prophecy of the Blessed Man Concerning the Din of Battles Fought At a Distance

AFTER the battle of Cooladrummon, as we have been told, and after a lapse of two years, at the time when the blessed man first sailed out to travel from Scotia (Ireland), on a certain day, at the very hour in which was fought that great battle in Scotia (Ireland), which is called in Scotic (Irish) Ondemone, the same man of God, then living in Britain. narrated everything in order in the presence of King Conall the son of Comgell, not only about the battle that was fought, but also about those kings to whom the Lord vouchsafed victory over their enemies, whose proper names are Ainmire son of Sedna, and the two sons of Mac Eire, Domhnall and Forcus. But the Saint moreover prophesied in like manner of the king of the Cruithne (Irish Picts) who was named Eochoid Laib, how when he was beaten he escaped, sitting in his chariot.

Chapter Eight - Of the Battle of the Miathi

AT another time, this is after many years had passed since the above-mentioned battle, while the holy man was in the Iouan island (Iona), suddenly he says to his attendant Diormit, 'Ring the bell.' The brethren, being stirred by the sound of this, make their way as fast as they can to the church, the holy abbot himself going before them. There he begins on bended knees to say to them, 'Now let us pray the Lord earnestly for this people and for King Aidan, for at this hour they are beginning the battle.' And after a moderate interval he goes out of the oratory, and looking up to heaven, he says, 'Now are the barbarians put to flight, and to Aidan is granted the victory, a sad one though it be.' But, further, the blessed man prophetically announced the number of the slain that were of Aidan's army, three hundred and three men.

Chapter Nine - Prophecy of St. Columba Concerning the Sons of King Aidan

AT another time, before the above-mentioned battle, the Saint questions King Aidan respecting his successor in the kingdom. On his replying that he does not know which of his three sons is to reign, whether Artur, or Eochoid Find, or Domingart, the Saint straightway prophesies on this wise: 'Not one of these three will be ruler, for they will fall in battles, being destined to be slain by their enemies; but now, if thou hast any younger sons, let them come to. me, and the one whom God will choose out of them as king will suddenly rush on to my lap.' And when they were called in, Eochoid Buide, according to the word of the Saint, came to him and lay in his bosom. And immediately the Saint kissed him, and blessed him, and says to his father, 'This is the survivor, and is to reign king after thee, and his sons will reign after him.' And so all things were afterwards completely fulfilled in their seasons. For Artur and Eochoid Find were slain, no long time after, in the above-mentioned battle of the Miathi; Domingart was slain in Saxonia (England) in the carnage of battle; but Eochoid Buide succeeded to the kingdom after his father.

Chapter Ten - Of Domhnall Son of Aedh

DOMHNALL son of Aedh, while yet a boy, was brought by his foster-parents to St. Columba in Drum Ceatt. And, looking upon him, he asks, saying, 'Whose son is this whom ye have brought unto me?' And when they answered, 'This is Domhnall son of Aedh, who has been brought unto thee with this object, that he may return enriched by thy blessing,' the Saint, when he has blessed him, straightway says, 'This one shall survive after all his brethren, and be a very famous king, nor shall he ever be delivered into the hands of his enemies, but shall die upon his bed, by a peaceful death, in old age, and in his own house, with a crowd of his familiar friends around him.' All which things were truly fulfilled according to the prophecy of the blessed man concerning him.

Chapter Eleven - Of Scandlan Son of Colman

AT the same time and place, the Saint goes to Scandlan son of Colman, then detained in bonds with King Aedh, being desirous to visit him; and, having blessed him, he comforted him and said: 'My son, be not sorrowful, but rather be glad and take courage, for King Aedh, with whom thou art in bonds, will depart from this world before thee, and, after some time of exile, thou art to reign for thirty years king in thine own nation. And again thou wilt be banished from thy kingdom, and wilt be an exile for some days, after which, recalled by the people, thou wilt reign for three short periods.' All which things were completely fulfilled according to the prophecy of the Saint. For after thirty years' time he was driven from the kingdom, and was an exile for a while; but afterwards, being recalled by the people, he reigned, not as he was expecting, for three years, but for three months (the 'three short periods'), after which he straightway died.

Chapter Twelve - A Prophecy of the Blessed Man Concerning Two Other Rulers, Who Were Called the Two Grandsons of Muiredach, Baitan Son of Mac Erce, and Eochoid Son of Domhnall

AT another time, while he was making his way through that rough and rocky region which is called Artdamuirchol (Ardnamurchan), and hearing his companions, namely, Laisran son of Feradach, and Diormit his attendant, conversing on the road about the two kings above mentioned, he addresses to them these words: 'O my children, why do you thus talk to no purpose of these men? For both those kings of whom you are now speaking have lately died, beheaded by their enemies. And, moreover, this very day will certain sailors airive from Scotia (Ireland), and tell you the very same about those kings.' And on the same day sailors from Ireland, arriving at the place called Muirbolc Paradisi (Port-na-Murloch), related to the two companions above mentioned, now sailing in the same ship with the Saint, the fulfilment of the prophecy of the venerable man, concerning those kings who were slain.

Chapter Thirteen - A Prophecy of the Holy Man Concerning Aengus Son of Aedh Comman

NOW this man, when banished from his own country with two other brethren, came as an exile to the Saint, who was then travelling in Britain, and he, blessing him, utters these prophetic words from his sacred breast: 'This youth shall remain a survivor after his other brothers are dead, and reign in the country for a long time, and his enemies shall fall before him, nor shall he ever be delivered into the hands of his enemies, but shall die in a good old age, by a peaceful death, surrounded by his friends.' All which things were completely fulfilled according to the word of the Saint. This is Aengus, whose surname was Bronbachal.

Chapter Fourteen - A Prophecy of the Blessed Man Concerning the Son of King Dermit, Who in the Scotic (Irish) Tongue Is Named Aedh Slane

AT another time, while the blessed man is staying for some days in Scotia (Ireland), he thus prophetically speaks to the above-mentioned Aedh, as he is coming up to him, and says, 'Thou oughtest to take care, my son, lest by committing a murderous deed thou losest the prerogative, predestined for thee by God, of being over-king of the whole realm of Ireland; for, if ever thou dost commit that crime, thou shalt not enjoy the whole kingdom of thy father, but only some part of it, in thine own tribe, and but for a short time.' Which words of the Saint were fulfilled exactly according to his prediction. For after he had killed Suibhne the son of Colman by treachery, not more, as is said, than four years and three months did he hold that part of the kingdom which had been conceded to him.

Chapter Fifteen - Prophecy of the Blessed Man Concerning King Rhydderch Son of Tudwal, Who Reigned on the Rock of Cluaith (Dumbarton)

THIS king at another time, being a friend of the holy man, sent some secret message to him by Lugbe Mocumin, desiring to know whether he was to be slain by his enemies or not. But Lugbe, being questioned by the Saint concerning that same king, and kingdom, and people, answers and says, as if pitying him, 'Why dost thou inquire about that unhappy man, who can in no way know in what hour he may be slain by his enemies?' Then the Saint says, 'He never will be delivered into the hands of his enemies, but will die in his own house, upon a feather pillow.' Which prophecy of the Saint concerning King Rhydderch was completely fulfilled, for, according to his word, he died by a peaceful death in his own house.

Chapter Sixteen - Prophecy of the Saint Regarding Two Boys, One of Whom Died at the End of the Week, According to the Saint's Word

AT another time, two countrymen come to the Saint, while he is dwelling in the Iouan island (Iona), one of whom, Meldan by name, asks the Saint about his son, who was present, what would happen to him in the future. To whom the Saint thus replies: 'Is not this day the Sabbath (Saturday)? Thy son will die on the sixth day (Friday), at the end of the week, and on the eighth day (from this), that is, on the Sabbath, he will be buried here.' Thereupon, notwithstanding this answer, the other countryman, named Glasderc, also asks about the son whom he had there with him, and receives the Saint's answer as follows: 'Thy son Ernane will see his descendants, and be buried in this island when an old man.' All which things, according to the word of the Saint, were completely fulfilled in due course in the case of both boys.

Chapter Seventeen - Prophecy of the Saint Regarding Colca Son of Aedh Draigniche, Who Was Descended From the Race of Fechureg, and Concerning a Certain Secret Sin of His Mother

AT another time, the Saint questions the above-mentioned Colca, who was staying with him in the Iouan island (Iona), about his mother, whether she was a religious woman or not. He says in reply, 'I know my mother to be well-conducted and of good report.' Then the Saint thus speaks prophetically: 'Set out at once for Scotia (Ireland), God willing, and question thy mother veiy closely concerning a certain very great secret sin of hers, which she is not willing to confess to any man.' And on hearing this he complied and went over to Ireland. Thereupon the mother, being closely questioned by him, although at first denying her sin, nevertheless confessed it, and, doing penance according to the judgement of the Saint, was healed (spiritually, and she greatly marvelled at what had been revealed to the Saint concerning her.

But Colca, having returned to the Saint, and stayed with him for some days, questioned him concerning the end of his own life, and received from the Saint this reply: 'In thine own country, which thou lovest, thou wilt be for many years superior of some church, and if perchance at any time thou seest thy cellarer making merry in a supper of his friends, and whirling round the bottle by its neck, know that in a short time thereafter thou wilt die.' What more need I say? This same prophecy of the blessed man was so fulfilled in all respects, as it had been prophesied concerning that same Colca.

Chapter Eighteen - Concerning Laisran the Gardener, a Holy Man

THE blessed man directed one of his monks named Trena, of the tribe Mac-Ui-Kuntir, to go out as his messenger to Scotia (Ireland) on a certain day. Who, obeying the command of the man of God, prepares in haste for the voyage, and complains in the presence of the Saint that he still wants one sailor. The Saint thereupon, in reply to him, utters these words from his sacred breast, saying, 'The sailor whom thou sayest is not yet at hand for thee, I cannot now find. Go in peace; until thou comest to Ireland thou wilt have fortunate and favourable winds. And whatsoever man thou shalt see from a distance coming to meet thee, who first of all the rest will seize the prow of thy ship in Ireland, this man will be the companion of thy journey in Ireland for some days, and will accompany thee on thy return thence to us; a man chosen of God, who in this my monastery will lead a holy life for all the rest of his time.' What more shall I say? Trena, receiving a blessing from the Saint, passed over all the seas with full sails, and, as he is nearing the haven of his ship, behold! Laisran Mocumoie runs up to him faster than the rest, and seizes the prow. The sailors recognize him as being the one of whom the Saint had foretold

Chapter Nineteen - How the Saint Knew Beforehand and Told of a Great Whale

ON a certain day, while the venerable man was living in the Iouan island (Iona), one of the brethren, Berachus by name, proposing to sail to the Ethican island (Tiree), came to the Saint in the morning and asked his blessing.

And the Saint looked upon him and said, 'my son, take great care to-day not to attempt to cross over in a direct course to the Ethican land by the wider sea, but rather go round about and sail by the smaller islands, lest, forsooth, terrified by some monstrous prodigy, thou shouldest scarcely be able to escape thence.' He, having received a blessing from the Saint, departed, got on board the ship, and set off, as if lightly regarding the word of the Saint. And thereupon, in passing over the wider reaches of the Ethican sea, he and the sailors who were with him look, and, behold, a whale of wondrous and immense size, lifting itself up like a mountain, while, floating on the surface, it opened wide its yawning mouth, all bristling with teeth. Then the rowers let down the sail, terribly alarmed, and, turning back, could scarcely escape from that tumult of the waves which arose from the motion of the monster, and, calling to mind the prophetic saying of the Saint, they greatly marvelled. The same day also, the Saint gave an intimation in the morning to Baithene, who was about to sail to the above-mentioned island, concerning the same whale, saying, 'In the middle of this last night a great whale has come up from the depths of the sea, and to-day it will lift itself up upon the surface of the ocean, between the Iouan and the Ethican islands.' Baithene answers him and says, 'That monster and I are under the power of God.' Then says the Saint, 'Go in peace, thy faith in Christ shall defend thee from this danger.' So Baithene, having received a blessing from the Saint, sails out from the port, and as soon as he and his companions have crossed over considerable reaches of sea, they behold the whale, and while all the rest are terribly alarmed, he alone is bold, and with both his hands upraised he blesses the sea and the whale. And in that very moment the huge monster dived under the waves, and no where appeared to them again.

Chapter Twenty - Prophecy of the Holy Man of a Certain Baitan, Who Had Sailed Out with Others, in Search of a Desert Island

AT another time one Baitan, by race a descendant of Niath Tolorg, asked to be blessed by the Saint, when about to seek, with others, a desert island. The Saint, as he bade him farewell, spoke this prophetic word concerning him: 'This man, who is setting out to seek a desert in the sea, will not lie buried in a desert, but will be buried in that place where a woman will drive sheep over his grave.' And so that same Baitan, after long wanderings over the stormy seas without finding a desert place, returned to his own land, and there remained for many years as the head of a small monastic house called in Scotic (Irish) Lathreginden. When after some time he died, and was buried in the Oak Grove of Galgach (Derry), it happened in those days that, on account of some hostile incursion, the common folk near to the church of the same place fled thereto, with their women and children. Whence it happened that one day a certain woman was observed driving her lambs over the grave of the same man, recently buried. And one of those who saw it, a holy priest, said, 'Now is fulfilled the prophecy of St. Columba, circulated many years ago.' Which above-mentioned presbyter, Mael-Odhrain by name, a soldier of Christ, of the clan Mocucurin, related these things to me, explaining in detail.

Chapter Twenty-One - Prophecy of the Holy Man Concerning One Neman, a Feigned Penitent

AT another time, the Saint comes to Hinba island, and the same day he directs that some indulgence of food should be allowed even to the penitents. Now there was there among the penitents one Neman, son of Cathir, who, though bidden by the Saint, refused to accept the proffered indulgence. So the Saint addresses him in these words: 'O Neman, dost thou not accept any indulgence of refreshment allowed by me and Baithene? A time will come when thou wilt secretly eat mare's flesh in a wood with robbers.' This same man then, having afterwards returned to the world, was found, according to the word of the Saint, eating such food, taken from a wooden grill, with robbers in a wood.

Chapter Twenty-Two - Of a Certain Wretched Man Who Slept With His Own Mother

AT another time, the Saint wakes up the brethren in the dead of night, and when they are gathered together in the church he says to them, 'Now let us pray to the Lord very earnestly, for in this hour some sin unheard of in the world has been perpetrated, and judicial retribution for it is greatly to be feared.' On the next day he spoke of this sin to a few who were asking about it, saying, 'After a few months that wretched creature will come to the Iouan island (Iona) with Lugaid, who knows nothing about it.' Accordingly, on another day, some months having passed, the Saint speaks to Diormit, saying: 'Rise quickly, behold, Lugaid is approaching, and tell him to put out that wretch, whom he has with him in the ship, on the Malean island (Mull), lest he should tread the sod of this island.' And he, following the direction of the Saint, goes to the sea, and tells Lugaid on his arrival all the words of the Saint concerning the wretched man. On hearing this, the poor wretch swore that he would never take food with others unless he could first see Columba, and speak with him. Diormit, returning to the Saint, related to him these words of the unhappy man. The Saint, on hearing them, went down to the port, and immediately said to Baithene, who was suggesting that the penitence of the unhappy man should be received, bringing forward testimonies of Holy Scripture, 'O Baithene, this man has been guilty of fratricide after the manner of Cain, and has committed adultery with his own mother.' Thereupon the miserable man promised on bended knees, on the shore, that he would fulfil the requirements of penance, according to the judgement of the Saint. And the Saint said to him, 'If for twelve years thou wilt do penance among the Britons, with weeping and tears, and not return to Scotia (Ireland) so long as thou livest, peradventure God will pardon thy sin.' Thus speaking, the Saint turns to his own people and says, 'This man is a son of perdition, who will not fulfil the penance which he has promised, but will soon return to Scotia (Ireland), and there he will shortly perish, slain by his enemies.' All which things so came to pass according to the prophecy of the Saint, for the wretched man, returning in those days to Ireland, fell into the hands of his enemies, and was slain in the region called Lea. He was of the race of Turtre.

Chapter Twenty-Three - Of the Vowel Letter I

ONE day Baithene conies up to the Saint, and says, 'I must have one of the brethren to run over with me and correct the Psalter which I have written.' On hearing which the Saint thus speaks: 'Why do you bring this trouble upon us without any occasion? For in this thy Psalter of which thou speakest there will not be found one letter over much nor another wanting, except the vowel I, which alone is wanting.' And so, when the whole Psalter had been read through, it was found on examination that what the Saint had said was true.

Chapter Twenty-Four - Of a Book That Fell Into a Water-Vessel, As the Saint Had Predicted

ONE day again, while, sitting at the hearth in the monastery, he sees Lugbe, of the tribe Mocumin, reading a book at a distance, to whom he suddenly says, 'Take care, my son, take care; for I think that the book which thou art reading is going to fall into a vessel full of water.' Which soon so happened, for that youth above mentioned, after some short time, rose to attend to something in the monastery, and forgot the word of the blessed man, so the book, which he carelessly held under his arm, suddenly fell into the vessel full of water.

Chapter Twenty-Five - Of a Horn of Ink, Foolishly Upset

ON another day, about the same time, shouting was heard on the other side of the Sound of the Iouan island (Iona); the Saint hearing the shouting while sitting in his cell that was raised on a platform, says, 'The man who is shouting across the Sound is not a person of delicate perception, for to-day, while bending over, he will upset my horn of ink.' His attendant Diormit, hearing this remark, stood for a little while at the gate, and waited for the troublesome guest who was coming, that he might keep watch over the ink-horn. But from some cause or other he soon went away, and after he had gone the dangerous guest arrived, and, in eager haste to kiss the Saint, upset the horn of ink, which was turned over by the edge of his garment.

Chapter Twenty-Six - Of the Arrival of a Guest of Some Importance, Whom the Saint Announced Beforehand

ANOTHER time, the Saint thus spoke to the brethren on a Tuesday: l Tomorrow, being Wednesday, we propose to fast, but yet, on the arrival of a certain dangerous guest, the customary fast will be relaxed.' Which so happened as had been foreshown to the Saint; for on the same Wednesday, in the morning, another stranger was shouting across the Sound, Aedhan by name, son of Fergno, who, as is said, ministered for twelve years to Brendan Mocualti; a very religious man he was, and he, when he arrived, relaxed the fast of that day, according to the word of the Saint.

Chapter Twenty-Seven - Of Some Man in Distress Who Was Shouting Across the Said Sound

AGAIN on a certain day, hearing some one shouting across the Sound, the Saint speaks on this wise: 'That man who is shouting is greatly to be pitied; he is coming to us in quest of some matters belonging to the healing of the body, whereas it were more fitting that he should exercise true repentance to-day for his sins, for in the close of this week he will die.' Which saying those who were present told to the unhappy man on his arrival. But he, lightly esteeming it, took what he had asked for, and quickly went back, and, according to the prophetic word of the Saint, before the end of the same week he died.

Chapter Twenty-Eight - Prophecy of the Holy Man of a City in Roman Jurisdiction Burnt By Sulphureous Fire That Fell Down from Heaven

AT another time again, Lugbe, of the tribe Mocumin, of whom we have made mention above, came one day to the Saint after the grinding of corn, and could in no wise look upon his face, overspread as it was with a wonderful flush; and being greatly alarmed he quickly fled. But the Saint, gently clapping his hands, calls him back. And being asked by the Saint immediately on his return why he had fled so fast, he gave this reply: 'I fled because I was very much afraid.' And after some little time, acting with more confidence, he ventures to question the Saint, saying, 'Has any awful vision been manifested unto thee in this hour?' The Saint made answer thus to him: 'So terrible a vengeance has now been wrought in a remote portion of the globe.' 'What manner of vengeance?' says the youth, 'and in what region wrought?' Then the Saint thus speaks: 'A sulphureous flame has in this hour been poured from heaven over a city of Roman jurisdiction, situated within the boundaries of Italy, and nearly three thousand men, not to mention a number of mothers and children, have perished. And before the present year is over, Gallic sailors, arriving from the provinces of the Gauls, will relate these same things to thee.' Which words were after some months proved to have been true sayings. For the same Lugbe, going in company with the holy man to the Land's Head (Cantyre), questioning the captain and sailors of a bark that arrived, hears narrated by them all those things about the city with its citizens, as they were predicted by the illustrious man.

Chapter Twenty-Nine - A Vision of the Blessed Max Concerning Laisran Son of Feradach

ON one very cold and wintry day the Saint wept, being afflicted by a great sorrow. His attendant Diormit, asking him about the cause of his sadness, received from him this reply: 'Not without reason, O my son, am I sorrowful in this hour, at the sight of my monks, whom Laisran is distressing during the construction of some greater building (round tower?), though they are even now worn out by heavy labour, a thing which greatly displeases me.' Wonderful to say! at that very moment of time, Laisran, dwelling in the monastery of Oakwood Plain (Durrow), in some way compelled, and as if kindled by some inward fire, orders that the monks cease from their labour, and that some refreshment of viands be prepared; and not only that they are to cease from work on that day, but to rest on other days of severe weather. The Saint, hearing in spirit these consolatory words spoken by Laisran to the brethren, ceased to weep, and, though himself dwelling in the Iouan island (Iona), related them throughout, with wondrous joy, to the brethren who were there at the time, and he blessed Laisran, the comforter of his monks.

Chapter Thirty - Of Feachna the Sage, How He Came as a Penitent to St. Columba, by Whom His Coming Was Foretold

AT another time the Saint, sitting on the top of a hill which overlooks from a distance this our monastery, turned to his attendant Diormit and spoke, saying, 'I wonder why a certain ship from Scotia (Ireland) is coming so slowly; it is bringing a certain sage who, having fallen in some wickedness, is going through a tearful repentance, and will soon be here.' Not long after that the attendant, looking towards the south, sees the sail of a ship drawing up to the port. And when he showed it to the Saint as it approached, he quickly rises, saying, 'Let us go to meet the stranger, whose true repentance Christ is accepting.' But Feachna gets down from the ship and runs up to meet the Saint on his way down to the port, and with weeping and lamentation, kneeling at his feet on bended knees, bewails his sins most bitterly, and confesses them before all who were there present. Then the Saint, weeping no less than he, says to him, 'Arise, my son, and be comforted; thy sins which thou hast committed are put away: for, as it is written, " A contrite and a humble heart God doth not despise."' And he arises, is joyfully received by the Saint, and after some days is sent to Baithene, then living as provost in the Plain of Lunge, and goes away in peace.

Chapter Thirty-One - Prophecy of the Holy Man about Cailtan, His Monk

AT another time, sending two monks to another monk of his named Cailtan, who at that time was provost in a cell which is now called by the name of his brother Diuni, close upon the lake of the river Aba (Loch Awe), the Saint sends by those messengers these words: 'Make haste and go quickly to Cailtan, and tell him to come to me without any delay.' And they obeyed the word of the Saint and went forth, and, arriving at Diuni's cell, informed Cailtan of the nature of their message. And he, in that same hour, without the least delay, followed the messengers of the Saint, and, accompanying them on their journey, quickly came to him, then dwelling in the louan island (Iona). On seeing him, the Saint thus speaks to him, and addresses him in these words: 'O Cailtan, thou hast done well in dutifully hastening to me; rest a while. It was for this reason that I, loving thee as a friend, sent to invite thee, that thou mayest finish the course of thy life in true obedience here with me. For before the end of this week thou wilt depart unto the Lord in peace.' On hearing which, he gives thanks to God, kisses the Saint with many tears, receives from him his benediction, and goes to the guest-house. And, falling sick the very night following, he passed away to Christ the Lord in the same week, according to the word of the Saint.

Chapter Thirty-Second - The Foresight and Prophecy of the Holy Man Concerning Two Brothers Who Were Strangers

ON a certain Lord's day, there was a shouting beyond the Sound which has so often been mentioned. The Saint, on hearing this shout, says to the brethren who were there, 'Go quickly, and bring at once the strangers who are coming to us from a distant land.' They, complying without delay, crossed the Sound and brought the guests, whom the Saint, when he had kissed them, straightway asks about the object of their journey. They answer and say, 'We are come that we may sojourn with thee even for this year.' To whom the Saint gave this reply: 'You will not be able to sojourn with me for the space of one year, as you say, unless you first undertake the monastic vow.' Those who were present greatly marvelled at this being said to guests only arriving in that very hour. In answer to these words of the Saint, the elder brother answers and says, 'Although up to this hour we never had this purpose in our minds, yet will we follow thy counsel, divinely inspired as we believe it to be.' Why say more? At that same moment of time they entered the oratory with the Saint, and devoutly, on bended knees, took the monastic vow. Then the Saint turns to the brethren, and says, 'These two strangers, offering themselves a living sacrifice to God, and in a short time fulfilling long years of Christian warfare, will soon, within this very month, pass over in peace to Christ the Lord.' On hearing which, both brothers, giving thanks to God, were led down to the guest-house, and in seven days' time the elder brother began to be sick, and at the end of the same week passed away to the Lord. Likewise also the other, falling sick after seven other days, happily passed to the Lord in the end of that week. And so, according to the true prophecy of the Saint, within the limit of the same month, both of them close this present life.

Chapter Thirty-Three - A Prophecy of the Holy Man Concerning One Artbranan

WHILE the blessed man was staying for some days in the Scian island (Skye), he struck with his staff a little spot of ground in a certain place near to the sea, and thus says to his companions, 'Wonderful to say, my sons! on this very spot of ground, a certain aged heathen, keeping the moral law of nature throughout his whole life, will this day be baptized, and will die, and will be buried.' And, behold, after about an hour's time a vessel arrived at the same port, in the forepart of which a certain decrepit old man was brought, the chief of the cohort of Geona, whom two youths lift out of the ship, and set down before the eyes of the blessed man. And he, receiving the word of God from the Saint through an interpreter, at once believed, and was baptized by him; and after the ministrations of baptism were completed, he thereupon died in the same place, and there his companions bury him, raising over him a heap of stones. And this is still to be seen on the seashore; and the river of the same place in which he had received baptism is even to this day called by the inhabitants, from his name, Dobur Artbranani.

Chapter Thirty-Four - Of a Boat That Was Moved At the Direction of the Saint

AT another time, while he was on a journey beyond the Backbone of Britain (Drum-Alban), and had found a certain little village among desert fields, the Saint there took up his quarters by the bank of a rivulet entering a lake; and the same night he wakes his sleeping companions, just half asleep, saying, 'Now! now! Quickly run out and bring hither directly our boat, which ye have put into a house on the other side of the stream, and put it in a house nearer to us.' They at once obeyed and did as they were told, but, while they were resting again, the Saint after some time quietly nudges Diormit, and says, 'Now! stand outside the house; see what is going on in that village where you first put our boat.' He, obeying the direction of the Saint, goes out of the house, and on looking he sees that the whole village is being burnt up in devouring flame, and so, returning to the Saint, he related to him what was going on there. The Saint then told the brethren about a certain envious adversary who had burnt those houses that very night.

Chapter Thirty-Five - Of Gallan Son of Fachtna, Who Was in the Jurisdiction of Colga Son of Cellach

ONE day again, the Saint, while sitting in his cell, speaks in prophecy to the same Colga, who is reading by his side, saying, 'Now are demons snatching away to hell an extortioner, one of the head men of thy jurisdiction.' But, on hearing this, Colga wrote down the time and hour on a tablet, and, when he returned after some months to his native country, he found, on inquiring of the inhabitants of that neighbourhood, that Gallan son of Fachtna had died at the very moment of time in which the blessed man told him of one snatched away by demons.

Chapter Thirty-Six - Prophecy of the Blessed Man of Findchan the Presbyter, the Founder of That Monastery Which in Scotic (Irish) is Called Artchain, in the Ethican Land (Tiree)

AT another time, the above-mentioned presbyter Findchan, a soldier of Christ, brought with him from Scotia (Ireland) into Britain, wearing the clerical habit, Aedh surnamed the Black, sprung of a royal race, a Cruthinian (Irish Pict) by nation, that he might sojourn with him in his monastery for some years. Now this Aedh the Black had indeed been a very bloody man and a murderer of many, and had even slain Diormit son of Cerbul, ordained by the will of Grod monarch of all Scotia (Ireland). This same Aedh then, after some time passed in the above sojourn, was ordained presbyter while with the above-named Findchan, a bishop having been summoned, although not rightly. The bishop, however, did not venture to lay a hand upon his head unless first Findchan himself, who loved Aedh 'after the flesh,' would place his right hand upon his head for a confirmation of the act. When such an ordination as this was afterwards made known to the holy man, he was much grieved; then straightway he utters this fearful sentence, concerning Findchan himself, and concerning Aedh who had been ordained, saying, 'That right hand which Findchan, contrary to law and ecclesiastical regulation, has laid on the head of a son of perdition, will soon rot, and, after great agonies of pain, will go before him to the earth for burial, and he will survive and live for many years after the burial of his hand. Aedh moreover, who was improperly ordained, will return like a dog to his vomit, will again be a bloody murderer, and at last, pierced by a lance, he will fall from wood into water, and die of drowning. Such an end of life he who murdered the monarch of all Scotia (Ireland) has long ago deserved.' Which prophecy of the blessed man was fulfilled in the case of both, for the right hand of the presbyter Findchan rotted through a blow, and went before him to the earth, being buried in that island which is called Ommon; but he himself, according to the word of St. Columba, lived for many years after. And Aedh the Black, a presbyter only in name, having returned to his former sins, was by craft pierced through with a lance, fell from the forepart of a ship into the water of a lake, and so perished.

Chapter Thirty-Seven - Of a Certain Consolation of the Holy Spirit Sent to the Monks By The Way, When They Were Wearied With Toil

AMONG these memorable utterances of the prophetic spirit, it seems not out of place also to make a record in our little narrative, of a certain spiritual consolation which on one occasion the monks of St. Columba perceived, when his spirit met them by the way. For on one occasion the brethren, re-turning to the monastery in the evening after their harvest work, and arriv-ing in that place which in Scotic (Irish) is named Cuuleilne, which place is said to be midway between the western plain of the Iouan island (Iona) and our monastery, they appeared each to feel within himself something wonder-ful and unusual, which, however, not one of them dared in any way to inti-mate to another. And so for some days they perceived it in the same place, and at the same evening hour. But in those days St. Baithene was the super-intendent of labours among them, and he thus spoke to them one day, saying, 'Now, brethren, if ye perceive any unusual and unexpected marvel in this place midway between the harvest-field and the monastery, ye ought each of you to declare it.' Then one of them, a senior, says, 'According to thy bidding I will tell what has been shown to me in this place; for in these days that are passing, and even now, I perceive some fragrance of wondrous odour, as if that of all flowers collected into one; also some burning as of fire, not penal, but somehow sweet; moreover also a certain unaccustomed and incompara-ble gladness diffused in my heart, which suddenly consoles me in a wonder-ful manner, and gladdens me to such a degree that I can remember no more the sadness, nor any labour. Yea, even the load, although a heavy one, which I am carrying on my back from this place until we come to the monastery, is so lightened, I know not how, that I do not perceive that I have a load at all.' What more shall I say? So all the harvest-workers declare, one by one, each for himself, that they have had sensations in all respects as one of them had narrated openly, and individually all together on bended knees besought of St. Baithene that he would take means to inform them, in their ignorance, of the cause and origin of the wondrous consolation which he and the rest were alike perceiving. To whom thereupon he gave this reply, saying, 'Ye know that our father Columba thinks anxiously about us, and takes it sadly that we come to him so late; but he being mindful of our labour, and by reason that he comes not to meet us in the body, his spirit meets our steps, and it is that which gladdens us with such consolations.' On hearing these words the brethren, still kneeling, with joy unspeakable, and with hands spread out to heaven, venerate Christ in the holy and blessed man.

But we ought not to be silent respecting this tradition concerning the voice of the blessed man in chanting the Psalms, which has undoubtedly been handed down from some who put it to the test. Which voice of the venerable man chanting in the church with the brethren, lifted up in a wonderful man-ner, was sometimes heard for four furlongs, that is, five hundred paces, but sometimes even for eight furlongs, that is, a thousand paces. Wonderful to relate! In the ears of those who were standing with him in the church, his voice did not exceed the ordinary measure of the human voice in loudness of tone. But yet at the same hour those who were standing more than a thou-sand paces off heard the same voice so distinctly that they could even distin-guish by the separate syllables what verses he was singing, for his voice sounded alike in the ears of those close at hand and of those who were listening at a distance. However, this miracle of the voice of the blessed man is not proved to have occurred always, but only on rare occasions, yet it could not have happened at all without the grace of the Divine Spirit.

But we must not be silent concerning what is said once to have taken place, in connexion with such wonderful elevation of his voice, close to the fortress of King Brude. For while the Saint himself, with a few brethren, was conducting after their manner the evening praises of God outside the king's fortress, some Druids, coming nearer to them, tried to hinder them as much as possible, that the voice of Divine praise proceeding from their mouth might not be heard among the heathen people. As soon as he found this out, the Saint began to sing the forty-fourth (45th) psalm, and in a wonderful manner his voice was at that moment so lifted up in the air, like some dreadful thunder, that both king and people were affrighted by terror too great to be endured.

Chapter Thirty-Eight - Of a Certain Rich Man Named Lugud Clodus

AT another time, while the Saint was staying in Scotia (Ireland) for some days, he saw another clerk mounted on a chariot, and gaily driving over the plain of Bregh (in Meath). First asking about him who he was, he received this answer concerning him from the man's friends: 'This is Lugud Clodus, a man who is rich, and honoured among the people.' The Saint thereupon answers and says, 'I do not so regard him, but rather as a poor wretched creature who on the day of his death will be retaining at his place in one enclosure three stray cattle of his neighbours; and of these strays he will order one selected cow to be killed for himself, and will ask for some part of her cooked flesh to be given to him, while he is lying in the same bed with a harlot. And as soon as he takes a bite out of that portion, he will be choked there and then, and will die.' All which things, as is related by well-informed persons, were fulfilled according to the prophetic word of the Saint.

Chapter Thirty-Nine - Prophecy of the Saint Concerning Neman Son of Gruthriche

FOR now, when the Saint reproved him for his evil deeds, he thought lightly of the Saint, and derided him. The blessed man answers him and says, 'In the Name of the Lord, Neman, I will speak some true words of thee. Thine enemies will find thee lying in the same bed with a harlot, and there wilt thou be slain. Demons also will carry off thy soul to the places of punishments.' This same Neman, being found after some years in the same bed with a harlot, in the region of Cainle (not identified), met with his end according to the word of the Saint, being beheaded by his enemies.

Chapter Forty - Prophecy of the Holy Man Concerning a Certain Presbyter

AT another time, while the Saint was staying in the country of the Scots (Irish) mentioned a little above, he came by chance on the Lord's day to a neighbouring monastery called in Scotic (Irish) Trioit (Trevet in Meath). The same day, hearing a presbyter celebrating the sacred mysteries of the Eucharist, one whom the brethren residing there had chosen to perform the solemnities of masses because they considered him to be very religious, he suddenly utters from his mouth this fearful speech: 'Clean and unclean things are now perceived to be equally mingled together, that is, the pure mysteries of the sacred offering are administered by an impure man, who meanwhile is hiding in his conscience a certain great crime.' Those who were within, hearing this, stood amazed, greatly terrified. But he of whom these words were said was constrained to confess his sin in the presence of all. And the fellow-soldiers of Christ, who stood around the Saint in the church, and heard him laying bare the hidden things of the heart, glorified the Divine knowledge in him, greatly wondering.

Chapter Forty-One - Prophecy of the Holy Man Concerning Erc Mocudruidi, a Robber, Who Dwelt in the Island of Colonsay

AT another time the Saint, while dwelling in the Iouan island (Iona), called to him two of the brethren, men whose names were Lugbe and Silnan, and gave them directions, saying, 'Now pass over to the Malean island (Mull), and in the fields near the sea seek out Ere, a robber, who last night came alone and secretly from the island of Colonsay, and through the day tries to hide himself under his coracle covered with hay, among the sand-hills, that by night he may sail over to the little island where the sea-calves (seals), that are ours by right, are bred and breed, that the greedy and most thievish fellow may fill his coracle with them when savagely slain, and then make his way back to his own home.' On hearing these words they obediently set out, and find the thief hidden in the places indicated by the Saint, and then they brought him to the Saint, as he had instructed them to do. On seeing him, the Saint says to him, 'Why dost thou often steal the goods of others, transgressing the Divine command? When thou art in need, come to us and thou shalt receive for the asking whatever is necessary.' And thus saying, he ordered sheep to be killed, and given to the wretched thief in place of the seals, lest he should return empty to his home. And after some time the Saint, foreseeing in spirit that the death of the thief was at hand, sends to Baithene, at that time dwelling in the Plain of Lunge (in Tiree) as manager, to send to the same thief a fat sheep and six pecks (of corn) as his last gifts. Which being sent over by Baithene as the Saint had directed, on that day the wretched thief was found overtaken by sudden death, and the presents that had been sent over were made use of at his funeral feast.

Chapter Forty-Two - A Prophecy of the Holy Man Concerning Cronan, a Bard

AT another time, while the Saint was sitting one day with the brethren near Lough Key, by the mouth of the river called in Latin Bos (the Boyle), a certain Scotic (Irish) bard came down to them; and when, after some conversation, he had gone away, the brethren say to the Saint, 'How was it that thou didst not call upon Cronan the Bard, when he was going away from us, for some song to be musically rendered after the manner of his art?' The Saint answered them, 'Wherefore do ye also now utter useless words? How could I ask for a song of joy from that unfortunate creature who even now, slain by his enemies, has so soon come to the end of his life?' No sooner had the Saint thus spoken, than, lo! some man shouts over the river, saying, 'That bard who has just returned from you safe and sound, has in this very hour been slain by his enemies on the road.' Then all who were present, greatly marvelling, looked in amazement one upon another.

Chapter Forty-Three - A Prediction of the Holy Man Regarding Two Chieftains, Who Perished By Wounds Mutually Inflicted

AT another time, when the Saint was living in the Iouan island (Iona), while he was reading, suddenly, in great amazement, he sighed in the very deepest sorrow. Seeing which, Lugbe Mocublai, who was present, began to inquire of him the cause of his sudden grief. To whom the Saint, in great sorrow, gave this reply: 'Two men of royal race in Scotia (Ireland) have just now perished, pierced by wounds mutually inflicted, not far from the monastery called Cellrois (Magheross in Monaghan) in the province of the Maugdorni (Cremorne and Farney), and on the eighth day, after this week has passed, another man will shout over the Sound, who, coming from Ireland, will tell of these deeds thus done. But, O my son, tell this to no man so long as I live.' Accordingly, on the eighth day, there was a shout over the Sound. Then the Saint, calling the above-named Lugbe to him, whispers to him, and says, 'He who is now shouting over the Sound is that aged traveller of whom I told thee before; go, and bring him to us.' And he, being quickly led up, among other things told this also, saying, 'Two men of noble birth in the province of the Maugdorni have died, inflicting mutual wounds, namely, Colman the Hound son of Ailen, and Ronan son of Aedh son of Colga, of the race of the Easterns (East Oriel), near the bounds of those places where stands the monastery called Cellrois.' After these words of that story, the same Lugbe, a soldier of Christ, began to question the Saint aside, saying, 'Tell me, I beseech thee, about these prophetic revelations, so wonderful as they are, how they are manifested to thee, whether by sight, or hearing, or in some other way unknown to men?' To this the Saint replies, 'Concerning that very subtle matter about which thou art now inquiring, I shall not be able to give thee any, even the very least intimation whatever, unless first, on bended knees, thou wilt promise me faithfully, by the Name of the High God, that thou wilt never communicate this most secret mystery to any man all the days of my life.' He then, hearing this, at once knelt down, and, with his face prostrated to the earth, fully promised everything according to the direction of the Saint. Which promise being promptly made, the Saint thus speaks to him as he rises: 'There are some, although very few, to whom Divine grace has granted this, that they can clearly and most distinctly see, at one and the same moment, as it were under a single ray of the sun, even the entire circuit of the whole earth, with its surrounding of sea and sky, the inmost recess of their mind being wondrously enlarged.' Although the Saint appears to relate this marvel of others of the elect, avoiding vainglory in every way, yet no one ought to doubt that he was speaking of himself, although by an indirect reference; no one, that is, who reads Paul the Apostle, that chosen vessel, speaking of such visions revealed to himself. For he did not write thus, 'I know myself,' but, 'I know a man, caught into the third heaven.' Which, although he appears to say it of another, yet no one doubts that he, preserving his humility, is so speaking of his own person.

Whom also our own Columba followed in the abovementioned narration of spiritual visions, which the aforesaid man, whom the Saint greatly loved, could scarcely extract from him even by strong entreaties beforehand, as he himself bore witness after the departure of St. Columba, before other holy men, from whom we have learned these things which we have above related undoubtingly, concerning the Saint.

Chapter Forty-Four - Of Cronan, a Bishop

AT another time, a certain stranger came to the Saint from the province of the Munster-men, and in his humility disguised himself as much as he could, that no one might know he was a bishop, but yet this could not be hidden from the Saint. For on one Lord's day, being requested by the Saint to prepare Christ's Body according to custom, he calls the Saint to him, that they may break the Lord's Bread together, as two presbyters. The Saint thereupon goes up to the altar, and, suddenly looking on his face, thus addresses him:

'Christ bless thee, brother; break this bread alone, by the episcopal rite; now we know that thou art a bishop. Wherefore hast thou thus far tried to disguise thyself, so that the veneration due to thee was not rendered unto thee by us?' On hearing this discourse of the Saint, the humble stranger, greatly astonished, worshipped Christ in the holy man, and those who were present, greatly wondering, glorified the Lord.

Chapter Forty-Five - A Prophecy of the Holy Man Concerning Ernan, a Presbyter

AT another time, the venerable man sent over Ernan, his uncle, an aged presbyter, to the headship of that monastery which he had founded in Hinba island (Eilean-na-Naoimh?) many years before. And so when the Saint blessed him and kissed him as he went out, he spoke this prophecy concerning him, saying, 'I do not hope again to see this my friend, now departing, alive in this world.' Accordingly the same Ernan, after not many days, being afflicted by some trouble, was at his own desire carried back to the Saint; who, greatly rejoicing at his arrival, began to go and meet him at the landing-place. Now Ernan himself, although with feeble, nevertheless his own, footsteps, was endeavouring with great alacrity to meet the Saint on the way from the harbour. But when there was a space of about four and twenty paces between the two, he, being overtaken by sudden death, and before the Saint could look upon his face in life, breathed his last and fell to the earth, that the word of the Saint might in no way fail of its effect. Wherefore in the same place a cross has been fixed in (a base) before the door of the kiln, and another cross stands in like manner, fixed in where the Saint stood still when Ernan died.

Chapter Forty-Six - A Prophecy of the Holy Man Concerning the Little Family of a Certain Peasant

ANOTHER time again, a certain peasant came among others to the Saint while staying in the district which is called in Scotic Coire Salchain (Corry in Morvern?). And when the Saint saw him coming to him in the evening, he asked, 'Where dwellest thou?' He says, 'I dwell in the district which borders on the shores of the lake Crogreth (Loch Creran?).' 'Savage marauders,' says the Saint, 'are now harrying that province of which thou speakest.' On hearing which the unhappy peasant began to bewail his wife and children. The Saint, seeing him very sorrowful, consoles him and says, 'Go, poor fellow, go; the whole of thy little family has escaped by fleeing to the mountain; but the invaders have driven off all thy little herd with them, and likewise cruel robbers have carried away all thy household goods along with the booty.' On hearing this the peasant returned to his own country, and found all things fulfilled exactly as predicted by the Saint.

Chapter Forty-Seven - A Prophecy of the Holy Man Concerning a Certain Peasant of the Name of Guire, Son of Aedhan

AT another time, a certain peasant, the bravest of all the men of that period among the people of Korkureti (Corkaree?), inquires of the holy man by what death he is to be overtaken. To whom the Saint says, 'Not in battle, nor on the sea, wilt thou die; the companion of thy journey, of whom thou hast no suspicion, will be the cause of thy death.' 'Perchance,' says Guire, 'some one of my friends who accompany me may design to kill me; or my wife, for the love of some younger man, may put me to death by foul play.' 'Not so,' says the Saint, 'will it happen.' 'Wherefore,' says Guire, 'art thou not willing now to inform me of my murderer?' 'For this reason,' says the Saint, 'I am unwilling now to tell thee anything more plainly about that thy dangerous companion, lest the frequent recollection of it being recalled should sadden thee overmuch, until the day comes in which thou wilt prove the truth of the same thing.' Why delay we with words? After some courses of years, the same Guire above mentioned, by chance one day sitting by a boat, was scraping the bark (or a knot?) from a spear-shaft with his own knife; then hearing others fighting among themselves near at hand, he quickly rises to separate them from their fighting, and, the same knife being carelessly left on the ground in that sudden movement, his knee was severely wounded by lighting on it. And now that such a companion brought it about, the cause of his death became manifest; and he himself, greatly impressed in his mind, at once recognized it, according to the prophecy of the holy man; and after some months, succumbing to that wound, he dies.

Chapter Forty-Eight - The Beautiful Foreknowledge of the Holy Man and His Prophesying Concerning another Thing Also, Which, Although a Minor Matter, Is Not, I Think, One to Be Passed Over in Silence

FOR, indeed, at another time, when the Saint was living in the Iouan island (Iona), he calls one of the brethren to him, and thus addresses him: 'On the third day from this that is breaking, thou oughtest to sit on the sea-shore, and look out in the western part of this island; for from the northern part of Ireland, a certain guest, a crane to wit, beaten by the winds during long and circuitous aerial flights, will arrive after the ninth hour of the day (3 p.m.), very weary and fatigued, and, its strength being almost gone, it will fall down before thee and lie on the beach. Thou wilt take care to lift it up tenderly, and carry it to some neighbouring house; and, while it is there hospitably received, thou wilt diligently feed it, attending to it for three days and three nights; and then, refreshed after the three days are fulfilled, and unwilling to sojourn any longer with us, it will return with fully recovered strength to its former sweet home in Scotia (Ireland) whence it came; and I so earnestly commend it to thee, because it comes from our fatherland.'

The brother obeys, and on the third day, after the ninth hour, as he had been bidden, he awaits the coming of the anticipated guest, and then, when it is come; fallen, he lifts it from the beach; weak, he bears it to the hospice; hungry, he feeds it. And when he has returned to the monastery in the evening, the Saint, not questioning, but declaring, says, 'God bless thee, my son, for that thou hast well attended to our stranger guest, which will not tarry long in its wanderings, but after three days will return to its native land.' Which the event also proved, just as the Saint predicted. For after being lodged for three days, it first lifted itself up on high by flying from the earth in the presence of its ministering host; then, after looking out its way in the air for a little while, it crossed the ocean wave, and returned to Ireland in a straight course of flight on a calm day.

Chapter Forty-Nine - The Foreknowledge of the Blessed Man Concerning the War Which Took Place after Many Years in the Fortress of Cethirn, and About a Certain Well Near to That Place

AT another time, when, after the conference of the kings, namely, Aedh the son of Ainmire, and Aidan the son of Gabran, the blessed man was returning to the watery plains, he and the abbot Comgell sit down not far from the above-mentioned fortress, on a bright summer's day. Then water is brought to the Saints in a brazen vessel from a spring hard by, for them to wash their hands. Which when St. Columba had received, he thus speaks to the abbot Comgell, who is sitting beside him: 'The day will come, O Comgell, when that spring, from which has come the water now brought to us, will not be fit for any human purposes.' 'By what cause,' says Comgell, 'will its spring water be corrupted?' Then says St. Columba, 'Because it will be filled with human blood, for my family friends and thy relations according to the flesh, that is, the Hy-Neill and the Pictish people, will wage war, fighting in this fortress of Cethirn close by. Whence in the above-named spring some poor fellow of my kindred will be slain, and the basin of the same spring will be filled with the blood of him that is slain with the rest.' Which true prophecy of his was fulfilled in its season after many years. In that same war, as many people know, Domhnall son of Aedh came off victorious, and in the same spring, according to the prophecy of the holy man, a certain man of his race was slain. Another soldier of Christ, Finan by name, who for many years irreproachably led an anchorite's life near the monastery of Oakwood Plain (Derry), relating some things about the same battle, which was fought while he was looking on, declared to me, Adamnan, that he saw the dead body in the above-mentioned spring; and that on the same day, on his return from the battle-field to the monastery of St. Comgell, called in Scotic (Irish) Cambas, for he had at first set out thence, he there found two aged monks of St. Comgell; to whom when he told some particulars of the battle fought before his eyes, and of the spring corrupted with human gore, they at once say, 'Columba was a true prophet, for he announced many years beforehand in our hearing, in the presence of St. Comgell, sitting near the fortress of Cethirn, that all these things, fulfilled to-day, which thou tellest of the battle and of the spring, would surely come to pass.

Chapter Fifty - Of the Distinction between Different Presents, Revealed to the Holy Man by Divine Grace

IN the same period Conall, bishop in Coleraine, collected well-nigh countless presents from the people of the plain of Eilne (between the rivers Bush and Bann), and prepared a hospitable reception for the blessed man on his return after the conference of the above-mentioned kings, with a great multitude following him. Then the many presents of the people, laid in the courtyard of the monastery, are given to the holy man to be blessed on his arrival. And while he is looking upon them as he blesses them, he specially points out the present of a certain rich man, and says, 'The mercy of God attendeth the man whose present this is, for his charities to the poor, and for his liberality.' And again he distinguishes another present among many others, saying, 'I can in no wise taste of this present of a wise man who is also avaricious, unless he first exercises true repentance for the sin of avarice.' Then Columb son of Aedh, conscious of his fault, and soon hearing this saying going about among the multitude, runs up and does penance before the Saint on bended knees, and promises that thenceforth he will renounce avarice; and that liberality shall follow, together with his amendment of character. And, being bidden by the Saint to rise, he was from that hour cured of the vice of a grasping disposition. For he was a wise man, as had been revealed to the Saint in his present. But that liberal rich man of the name of Brendan, of whose present we have spoken a little above, himself also hearing the words of the Saint spoken concerning him, kneels at the feet of the Saint, and implores that the Saint will pour out prayer for him to the Lord. Then, being first reproved by him (the Saint) for certain sins of his, he exercised repentance, and promised to amend thenceforth. And so each one was amended and cured of his own special vices.

With like knowledge the Saint also at another time recognized the present of a certain grasping man, named Diormit, among many other presents collected on his arrival at the Great Cell of Deathrib (Kilmore in Roscommon?).

It may be enough to have written these things concerning the prophetic grace of the blessed man, a few out of many, as it were, in the text of this first book. Few, I say; for this is not to be doubted of the venerable man, that there may have been holy secrets hidden within, which in no wise could come to the knowledge of men, far more numerous than those which, like some little droppings at times, escaped as if through a few fissures of some vessel full of most actively fermenting new wine. For holy and apostolic men, avoiding vainglory, for the most part, and so far as they are able, are quick to conceal some internal secrets that are inwardly shown to them by God. But God makes manifest some of those, whether they themselves will or not, and in some way brings them out, willing indeed to honour those Saints who honour Him, that is, the Lord Himself, to Whom be glory for ever and ever.

Here we make an end of this first book; now in the next place begins the book of his miraculous powers, which are for the most part also associated with prophetic foreknowledge.

The Second Book, of Miracles of Power

Chapter One - Of the Wine That Was Made Out of Water

AT another time, when the venerable man was staying in Scotia (Ireland) with St. Findbar (Finnian) the bishop, while he was yet a youth, learning the wisdom of Holy Scripture, on a certain solemn day the wine for the sacrificial mystery, by some chance, was not found. And when he heard the ministers of the altar complaining among themselves of the want of it, he, as deacon, takes a pitcher and goes to the spring, to draw spring water for the ministrations of the Holy Eucharist, for in those days he was ministering in the order of the diaconate. And so the blessed man in faith blessed the watery element which he drew from the spring, calling on the name of the Lord Jesus Christ, who in Cana of Galilee turned water into wine, who also working in this miracle, the inferior, that is, the watery nature, was by the hands of the famous man converted into the more agreeable species, that namely of wine. And so the holy man, returning from the spring and entering the church, places by the altar the pitcher having within it such liquid; and says to the ministers, 'Ye have wine, which the Lord Jesus has sent for the execution of His mysteries.' When they understood this, the holy bishop with the ministers together give great thanks to God. But the holy youth ascribed this not to himself, but to the holy bishop Vinnian (Finnian). And so Christ the Lord manifested this first proof of power by His disciple, which He wrought by Himself in the same case, placing it as the beginning of miracles in Cana of Galilee.

Let the beginning, I say, of this little book, as if it were some lamp, make it clear that a Divine miracle was manifested through our Columba; that we may next pass on to other miracles of power which were shown through him.

Chapter Two - Of the Rough-Flavoured Fruit of a Certain Tree Which Was Turned Into Sweetness by the Blessing of the Saint

THERE was a certain tree very full of apples near the monastery of Oakwood Plain (Derry), in the southern part of it, and when the inhabitants of the place made some complaint about the excessively rough flavour of the fruit, one day in the autumn season the Saint went up to it, and seeing that the tree in vain bore abundant fruits which afflicted rather than delighted those who tasted any of them, raises his holy hand and blesses it, saying, 'In the name of Almighty God let all thy roughness, rough-tasting tree, depart from thee, and let thine apples, up to this time most roughly flavoured, be turned into the very sweetest.' Wonderful to say, and sooner than said, in the

46

same moment, all the apples of that tree lost their roughness of flavour, and, according to the word of the Saint, were turned to a wondrous sweetness.

Chapter Three - Of a Corn-Field Sown After the Middle Time of Summer, and Reaped in the Beginning of the Month of August, at the Prayer of the Saint When He Lived in the Iouan Island (Iona)

AT another time the Saint sent his monks to bring faggots from the field of a certain peasant, for the construction of a hospice. And when they came back to the Saint with their transport ship filled with the aforesaid cargo of twigs, and said that the peasant was very much distressed indeed on account of the loss of them, the Saint at once gives directions and says, 'Then lest we should put a stumbling-block in that man's way, let there be taken to him from us twice three (pecks) of barley, and let him sow it at once in his ploughed land. And when, according to the bidding of the Saint, it was sent to the peasant, Findchan by name, and set before him with such a commendation, he thankfully accepts it, but says, 'How can a field do any good if sown after midsummer, contrary to the nature of this land?' His wife, on the other hand, says, 'Do according to the command of the Saint, to whom the Lord will grant whatsoever he may ask of Him.' But they that were sent added this also at the same time, saying, 'St. Columba, who hath sent us to thee with this present, entrusted also this instruction through us about thy field, saying, "Let that man trust in the omnipotence of God: his field, although sown after twelve days of the month of June have passed, will be reaped in the beginning of the month of August."' The peasant obeys, both ploughing and sowing, and the harvest which he sowed against hope at the aforesaid time, he got in ripe in the beginning of the month of August, to the great admiration of all the neighbours, according to the word of the Saint, in the portion of land which is called Delcros (not identified).

Chapter Four - Of a Pestiferous Cloud, and the Healing of Many

AT another time, while the Saint was living in the Iouan island (Iona), sitting on the hill called in Latin Munitio Magna (Dun-bhuirg?), he sees in the north a dense and watery cloud arising from the sea on a clear day; which being seen as it rose, the Saint says to one of his monks, who was sitting beside him, Silnan by name, son of Nemandon Mocusogin, 'This cloud will be very baleful to men and cattle, and after rapidly flying this day over a great part of Scotia (Ireland), that is, from the river called Ailbine (Delvin) as far as the ford Clied (Ath Cliath, now Dublin), will in the evening rain down a pestiferous shower, which will cause grievous and purulent ulcers to be formed on the bodies of men and on the teats of cattle, from which the diseased men and cattle will suffer, being afflicted by that poisonous disease even unto death. But we ought to have compassion upon them and relieve their suffering, the Lord being merciful. Do thou therefore, Silnan, now go down with me from the hill, prepare to sail to-morrow, if we live and God will, with, bread received from me and blessed by the invocation of the Name of God, which being put in water, men, and cattle also, sprinkled with that, will speedily recover their health.' Why do we linger over it? On the morrow Silnan quickly got ready whatever things were necessary, received from the hand of the Saint the blessed bread, and sailed forth in peace. And as he is departing from him in that same hour, the Saint adds this word of consolation, saying, 'Be assured, my son, thou wilt have favourable and prosperous winds day and night, until thou comest to that region which is called Ard Ceannachte (in Meath), that there thou mayest quickly relieve the sick with the healing bread.' Why say more? Silnan obeyed the word of the Saint, and with the Lord's help, arriving by a prosperous and speedy voyage to the above-mentioned part of that district, found the people of whom the Saint had foretold, devastated by the pestiferous shower of the aforesaid cloud, that so quickly rushed on before him, raining upon them. And in the first place, twice three men, in the same house near the sea, being found placed in the last extremity with death at hand, being sprinkled by the same Silnan with the water of benediction, in the self-same day were opportunely healed. The rumour of this rapid cure being quickly carried about through all the district wasted by that very pestilential disease, summoned all the people who were diseased to the messenger of St. Columba; who, according to the command of the Saint, sprinkled men and cattle with water containing blessed bread; and the men, at once recovering perfect health, preserved together with their cattle, praised Christ in St. Columba with high thanksgiving. And so, in this narrative above recorded, these two things, as I think, are manifestly associated in equal measure, namely, the grace of prophecy concerning the cloud, and the miracle of power in the healing of the sick. That these things are in all respects most true, the above-mentioned Silnan, soldier of Christ and messenger of St. Columba, witnessed before Seghine the abbot and other aged men.

Chapter Five - Of Maugina Daughter of Daimen, a Holy Virgin, Who Had Dwelt in Clocher (Clogher) of the Sons of Daimen

AT another time the Saint, while he was living in the Iouan island (Iona), at the first hour of the day calls to him a certain brother, Lugaid by name, whose surname in Scotic (Irish) is Lathir, and thus addresses him, saying, 'Make ready quickly for a hasty voyage to Scotia (Ireland), for it is very necessary for me to send thee as a messenger to Clocher of the sons of Daimen (Clogher). For in this last night Maugina, a holy virgin, a daughter of Daimen, returning home from the oratory after mass evensong), by some chance has taken a false step, and her hip is broken in twain. This woman in her cries is often calling my name to remembrance, hoping that through me she will receive comfort from the Lord.' Why more? As Lugaid is obeying, and straightway setting out, the Saint hands to him a little box of pine-wood containing a blessed gift, saying, 'Let the blessed gift contained in this little box, when thou comest to visit Maugina, be put into a vessel of water, and let the same water, of blessing be poured over her hip: and immediately, on calling upon the name of God, the hipbone will be joined and united, and the holy virgin will recover perfect health.' And the Saint adds these words: 'Behold! I do now in person write in the cover of this box the number of twenty-three years, during which the holy virgin is to live in this present life after the same cure.' All which things were thus completely fulfilled, as predicted by the Saint; for, as soon as Lugaid came to the holy virgin, and her hip was bathed, as the Saint recommended, with the blessed water, the bone was united without any, even the least, delay, and she was completely cured; and, rejoicing in the coming of the messenger of St. Columba with great thanksgiving, lived, according to the prophecy of the Saint, for twenty-three years after her cure, continuing in good works.

Chapter Six - Of the Cures of Divers Diseases, Which Were Performed In Drum Ceatt

THE man of illustrious life, as has been related to us by persons of experience, healed the sicknesses of divers persons by calling on the name of Christ, in those days when he went to the conference of kings in Drum Ceatt, and abode there for a short season. For many sick persons, either by the stretching forth of his holy hand, or being sprinkled with water blessed by him, or even by the touch of the border of his garment, or of anything, salt for instance, or bread that had received his benediction and been put in water, believing, recovered perfect health.

Chapter Seven - Of a Piece of Rock-Salt Blessed By the Saint, Which the Fire Could Not Consume

AT another time, Colga the son of Cellach received from the Saint a piece of rock-salt that had been blessed, and for which he had asked, for the benefit of his sister who had brought him up, and who was suffering from a very severe attack of inflamed eyes. The same sister and nurse, taking such a blessed gift from the hand of her brother, hung it up on the wall over the bed;

and by chance it happened after some days that the same village, with the cottage of the above-mentioned woman, was wholly burnt up by the devastating flame. Wonderful to say, a small part of that wall, lest the blessed man's blessed gift that was hung on it should perish, remained standing unhurt after the whole of the house was burnt, nor did the fire dare to touch the two stakes on which was hanging the piece of rock-salt.

Chapter Eight - Of a Book-Leaf Written By the Hand of the Saint, Which Could Not Be Injured by Water

ANOTHER miracle, which was at one time wrought by means of the opposite element, should not, I think, be passed over in silence. For, when the courses of many years had rolled by after the passing to the Lord of the blessed man, a certain youth fell from his horse in the river which is called in Scotic (Irish) Boend (Boyne) and sank and died, and remained under the water for twenty days; he, as he had books enclosed in a leathern satchel under his armpit, and thus falling, was also found so, after the above-mentioned number of days, holding between his arm and his side the satchel with the books; and when his dead body was brought to the dry ground, and the satchel opened, a leaf written by the holy fingers of St. Columba was found dry and in no wise corrupted, as if it had been kept in a casket, among the leaves of other books that were not only corrupted but even putrefied.

Chapter Nine - Of another Miracle Wrought in a Like Case

AT another time, a book of hymns for the week written by St. Columba's own hand, together with the leathern satchel in which it was contained, fell from the shoulders of a certain boy who slipped off a bridge and was drowned in a certain river of the province of Leinster. Which little book, remaining in the water from the Nativity of Our Lord to the end of Easter week, and afterwards found on the bank of the river by some women who were walking there, is carried in the same satchel, which was not only wet but putrefied, to one Iogenan, a presbyter, and a Pict by nation, to whom it had previously belonged. And when the same Iogenan opened the satchel, he found his little book uncorrupted, and as clean and dry as if it had remained all that time in a case, and had never fallen into the water. But we have learned without doubt from men of experience that other like things occurred with respect to books written by the hand of St. Columba, which books, be it known, being immersed in water, could in no way be corrupted. But concerning the above-mentioned genuine book of Iogenan, we have received the account without any uncertainty from certain truthful, excellent, and trustworthy men, who have examined the same little book, which, after so many days of submersion as are above stated, was most white and clear.

These two miracles, although wrought in matters of small moment, and manifested through contrary elements, namely, fire and water, bear witness to the honour of the blessed man, and of how great arid of what manner of merit he was accounted in the sight of the Lord.

Chapter Ten - Of Water which was Brought Forth from the Hard Rock at the Prayer of the Saint

AND now, seeing that mention has been made a little above of the element of water, we ought not to be silent as to other miracles also which the Lord wrought, although at different times and places, in the case of the same created thing. For on another occasion, while the Saint is engaged in travelling, as he goes on his way, an infant is presented to him by its parents to be baptized; and because no water was found in the places close at hand, the Saint, turning aside to the nearest rock, prayed for a little while on bended knees, and, rising from his prayer, blessed the face of that same rock, from which thereupon water flowed, gushing out abundantly, in which he at once baptized the infant. Concerning whom also, when he had been baptized, he prophesied and spoke these words, saying, 'This long-lived little boy will live even to extreme old age; in his youthful years he will sufficiently serve the desires of the flesh, and in the next place will be devoted to the Christian warfare even to his life's end, and will pass away to the Lord in a good old age.' All which things happened to the same man according to the prediction of the Saint. This was Lugucencalad, whose parents were in Artdaib Muirchol (Ardnamurchan), where is seen at the present day a well, potent in the name of St. Columba.

Chapter Eleven - Of Other Spring Water of Malignant Quality, Blessed by the Blessed Man in the Country of the Picts

AT another time, the blessed man, while he was sojourning in the province of the Picts for some days, heard among the heathen people that a report was spread abroad concerning another spring, which senseless men, the devil blinding their understandings, worshipped as a god. For those who drank of the same spring, or purposely washed their hands or feet in it, being by God's permission smitten by demoniacal artifice, returned either leprous, or purblind, or certainly weak, or attacked by some other maladies, on account of all which things the heathen men were led astray, and rendered divine honour to the spring. On finding that these things were so, the Saint one day went boldly up to the spring, at the sight of which the Druids, whom he himself had often sent away confounded and vanquished by him, greatly rejoiced, thinking indeed that he would suffer similar things from the touch of that noxious water. But he, first lifting up his holy hand, with invocation of the Name of Christ, washes his hands and feet, and then, together with his companions, drinks of the same water that had been blessed by him. And from that day the demons departed from that spring; and not only was it not permitted to injure any one, but even, after the blessing of the Saint and his washing therein, many diseases among the people were healed by the same spring.

Chapter Twelve - Of the Danger of the Blessed Man on the Sea, and of the Sudden Calming of the Storm When He Prayed

AT another time, the holy man began to be in peril by the sea, for the entire hull of the ship was heavily struck, and violently dashed about on the huge mountains of the waves, while a great tempest of winds bore upon them on every side. Then by chance the sailors say to the Saint as he is endeavouring with them to empty the bilge-hole, 'What thou now doest doth not greatly profit us in our danger; thou shouldest rather pray for us now that we are perishing.' On hearing which, he ceases to empty out the bitter water, the green sea-wave, but begins to pour out sweet and earnest prayer to the Lord. Wondrous to say, in the same moment of time in which the Saint, standing at the prow with his hands stretched out to heaven, besought the Almighty, the whole storm of wind and the raging of the sea, being stilled more quickly than can be said, ceased, and at once there followed a most tranquil calm. But they who were in the ship were amazed, and, rendering thanks with great wonder, glorified the Lord in the holy and famous man.

Chapter Thirteen - Of another Similar Peril to Him by the Sea

AT another time again, when a cruel and dangerous tempest was pressing heavily on them, and his companions were crying out for the Saint to beseech the Lord for them, he gave them this answer, saying, 'On this day it is not my lot to pray for you who are placed in this danger, but it is that of the abbot Cainnech, a holy man.' I am going to relate wonderful things. At that same hour St. Cainnech, living in his monastery, which in Latin is called Campulus Bovis, but in Scotic (Irish) Ached-bou (Aghaboe), the Holy Spirit revealing it to him, heard with the inward ear of his heart the above-mentioned saying of St. Columba; and when by chance he had begun after the ninth hour to break the holy-bread in the refectory, he quickly leaves the table, and , with one shoe clinging to his foot, while in his great haste the other was left behind, he hurriedly makes his way to the church, saying as he goes, 'It is not for us to dine now, at a time when the ship of St. Columba is in peril by the sea. For even now is he frequently calling on the name of this Cainnech, that he may pray Christ for him and his companions in peril.' Entering the oratory after these his words, he prayed for a little while on bended knees, and, the Lord hearing his prayer, the tempest straightway ceased, and the sea became very tranquil. Then in the next place, St. Columba, seeing in spirit Cainnech 's hastening to the church, although he was living so far away, wonderfully utters this sentence from his pure breast, saying, 'Now I know, O Cainnech, that God hath heard thy prayer, now doth thy rapid race to the church with one shoe greatly profit us.' In such a miracle as this, the prayer of both holy men, as we believe, had a joint effect.

Chapter Fourteen - Of the Staff of Saint Cainnech, Forgotten at the Harbour

AT another time, the same Cainnech who is mentioned above, when beginning to sail from the harbour of the Iouan island (Iona) to Scotia (Ireland), forgot to take his staff with him; which staff of his, indeed, being found on the shore after his departure, was put into the hand of St. Columba, and which, on his return home, he carries into the oratory, and there he remains some time alone in prayer. Cainnech then approaching the Oidechan island (Islay?), suddenly pricked to the heart for his forgetfulness, was inwardly cast down. But after some little time he got down from the ship, and , kneeling down in prayer on the land, found in front of him, upon the turf of the little land of Aithche, the staff which he had forgotten and left behind him at the harbour of the Iouan island. At its being thus carried out for him by the agency of Divine power, he greatly marveled, with giving of thanks in God (*in Deo*).

Chapter Fifteen - Of Baithene and Columban Son of Beogna, Holy Presbyters, Who ask that on the Same Day a Favourable Wind May Be Granted Them by the Lord Through the Prayer of the Blessed Man, Although they are Sailing Different Ways

AT another time again, the above-mentioned holy men coming to the Saint, with one consent ask of him at the same time, that he will ask and obtain from the Lord, that on the following day a favourable wind may be given to them, though they are outward bound in different directions. To whom the Saint answered and gave this reply: 'To-morrow morning Baithene, sailing out of the harbour of the Iouan island (Iona), will have a favourable breeze until he come to the harbour of the Plain of Lunge' (in Tiree). Which the Lord so granted, according to the word of the Saint, for the same day Baithene crossed with full sails the whole of the great sea even to the Ethican land (Tiree). But at the third hour of the same day the venerable man calls the presbyter Columban to him, saying, 'Now hath Baithene happily arrived at the desired haven: prepare thyself to sail to-day; soon will the Lord change the wind into the north.' At the same hour the south wind, obeying the word of the blessed man thus spoken, veers round into a northern breeze; and so on the same day each holy man, turning away the one from the other in peace, went out with full sails and favouring breezes; Baithene in the morning to the Ethican land, Columban in the afternoon beginning to make for Ireland. This miracle was effected, the Lord granting it, by the power of the prayers of the illustrious man, for, as it is written, 'All things are possible to him that believeth.' After the departure of St. Columban on that day, St. Columba uttered this prophetic saying concerning him: 'The holy man Columban, whom we blessed as he went out, will nowhere see my face in this world.' Which was thus fulfilled afterwards, for in the same year St. Columba passed away to the Lord.

Chapter Sixteen - Of the Driving Away of a Demon That Lurked in a Milk-Pail

AT another time a certain youth, Columban by name, of the race of Briun, suddenly came and stood at the door of the cell in which the blessed man was writing. This same youth, having returned from milking the cows, and carrying on his back the pail full of new milk, speaks to the Saint, that, according to custom, he may bless such a load. The Saint, being at some distance opposite to him, raised his hand, and formed the saving sign in the air, which then and there was greatly agitated, and the bar of the lid, driven through its two holes, was shot away to some distance; the lid fell to the ground, and most of the milk was spilled on the soil. The young lad then sets down the vessel on its bottom on the ground, with what little of the milk there was left, and kneels as a suppliant. To whom the Saint says, 'Arise, Columban! Thou hast done carelessly in thy work to-day; for thou hast not cast out the demon that was lurking in the bottom of the empty pail, by tracing on it, before pouring in the milk, the sign of the Lord's cross; and now not enduring, thou seest, the virtue of that sign, he has quickly fled away in terror, while at the same time the whole of the vessel has been violently shaken, and the milk spilled. Bring then the pail nearer to me, that I may bless it.' Which being done, the half-empty vessel that the Saint had blessed, was in the same moment found to be filled by Divine power, and what little had before remained in the bottom of the vessel, quickly rose up to the top under the benediction of his holy hand.

Chapter Seventeen - Of a Pail Which a Certain Sorcerer Named Silnan Had Filled with Milk Taken From a Bull

THIS is handed down as having been done in the house of a certain rich peasant, Foirtgirn by name, who was living in Mount Cainle (not identified). While the Saint was being lodged there, he judged with righteous judgement between two contending rustics, whose coming he knew beforehand, and one of them, a sorcerer, being bidden by the Saint, by his diabolical art took milk from a bull which was near at hand; which thing the Saint directed to be done, not to encourage those sorceries, far from it, but to destroy them in the presence of the multitude. The blessed man therefore asked that the vessel, full, as it seemed to be, of such milk, might be at once given to him, and with this sentence he blessed it, saying, 'Now it shall be proved that this, which is supposed to be true milk, is not so, but is blood deprived of its colour by the fraud of demons to deceive men;' and straightway that milky colour was turned into its own proper quality, that is, into blood. The bull also, which for the space of one hour was at death's door, wasting and worn by a horrible emaciation, on being sprinkled with water blessed by the Saint, was cured with wonderful rapidity.

Chapter Eighteen - Of Luqne Mocumin

ONE day, a certain youth of good disposition, Lugne by name, who afterwards when an old man was prior in the monastery of Elena island (one of the Garvelochs, or else Naomh, near Islay?), comes to the Saint, and complains of a flow of blood, which for many months was frequently issuing profusely from his nostrils. The Saint called him to come nearer, and blessed him, compressing both his nostrils with two fingers of his right hand. And from that hour of blessing, even to his dying day, blood never dropped from his nose.

Chapter Nineteen - Of Fishes Specially Prepared by God for the Blessed Man

AT another time, when some companions of the famous man, keen fishermen, had taken five fishes in a net in the fishful river Sale (Blackwater in Meath?), the Saint says to them, 'Cast your net a second time into the river, and immediately you will find a great fish, which the Lord hath prepared for me.' They, obeying the word of the Saint, drew forth in the net a salmon of wondrous size prepared for him by God. At another time again, while the Saint was staying for some days near Lough Ce (Key), he stopped his companions when they wanted to go a-fishing, saying, 'To-day and to-morrow not a fish will be found in the river; I will send you on the third day, and you will find two great river salmon caught in the net.' And so they, after two days, casting the net, drew to the land two, of most unusual size, which they found in the river called Bo (Boyle). In these two fishings that have been mentioned, the power of miracle appears, together with prophetic fore-knowledge accompanying it; for which things the Saint and his companions rendered special thanks to God.

Chapter Twenty - Of Nesan the Hunchback, Who Lived in the Country Bordering on the Lake Aporum (Lochaber)

THIS Nesan, when he was very poor, joyfully received the holy man on one occasion as his guest. And when he had entertained him hospitably, according to his means, for the space of one night, the Saint inquires of him how many little cows he had; he says, 'Five.' The Saint thereupon says, 'Bring them to me that I may bless them.' And when they were brought to him, and blessed with the lifting up of his holy hand, the Saint says, 'From this day thy few little cows, only five, shall increase even to the number of one hundred and five cows.' And because the same Nesan was a peasant man, with a wife and children, the blessed man conferred on him also this increase of benediction, saying, 'Thy seed shall be blessed in children and in grandchildren.' All which things were completely fulfilled, according to the word of the Saint, without any diminution.

[*Added in MS.* B. Of a certain rich but most grasping man named Uigene, who had despised St. Columba, and not received him as a guest, he uttered on the contrary this prophetic sentence, saying, 'But the riches of that avaricious man, who has spurned Christ in stranger guests, from this day shall be gradually diminished, and be reduced to nothing; and he himself will be a beggar, and his son will run about from house to house with a half-empty bag, and, struck with an axe by some rival in the pit of a threshing-floor, he will die.' All which things, according to the prophecy of the holy man, were completely fulfilled with respect both to the one and to the other.]

Chapter Twenty-One - Of Columban, a Man of Equally Humble Condition, Whose Cattle the Holy Man Blessed While Very Few in Number, but which after His Benediction Increased Even to the Number of One Hundred

AT another time again, the blessed man on a certain night was well lodged with the above-mentioned Columban, at that time a poor man, and, first thing in the morning, the Saint, as has been mentioned above in the case of Nesan, questions his peasant host as to the quantity and quality of his substance. Who on being questioned says, 'I have only five little cows, but they will increase to more if thou wilt bless them.' There and then, at the bidding of the Saint, he brought them to him, and in like manner, as has been said above of the five little cows of Nesan, he gives an equal blessing to the five little cows of this Columban, and says, 'One hundred and five cows, by the gift of God, shalt thou have, and in thy children and in thy posterity shall be a beautiful benediction.' All which things were most abundantly fulfilled, according to the prophecy of the blessed man, in his fields, in his cattle, and in his off-spring; and in a wonderful manner the number assigned beforehand by the Saint to the two men above mentioned, when fulfilled in the number of one hundred and five cows, could in no wise be added to; for whatever exceeded the number as limited above, being carried off by divers accidents, were no-where forthcoming, except what could be employed for the particular uses of the family, or else for the purpose of almsgiving. And so in this narrative, as in others, a miracle of power is openly showed together with prophecy: for in the great increase of the cows appears equally the virtue of benediction and of prayer, and, in the previous limitation of the number, prophetic fore-knowledge.

Chapter Twenty-Two - Of the Death of Evil-Doers Who Had Despised the Saint

THE venerable man greatly loved the above-mentioned Columban, whom the virtue of his benediction made rich from having been a poor man, be-cause he rendered to him many offices of kindness. Now there was at that time a certain man, an evil-doer, a persecutor of good men, named Ioan son of Conall son of Domhnall, sprung of the royal race of Gabhran. This man per-secuted the above-mentioned Columban, the friend of St. Columba, and laid waste his homestead, carrying off everything that could be found therein, acting in this hostile fashion not once only, but twice. Whence by chance it happened, and not undeservedly, to that evil-natured man, that on a third occasion, after a third harrying of that same homestead, while returning lad-en with spoil to the ship, together with his comrades, he had, straight before him, drawing nearer to him, the blessed man whom he had, as it were, des-pised at a distance. Arid when the Saint reproved him for his evil deeds, and would persuade him, begging him to lay down the spoil, he, remaining savage and not to be persuaded, despised the Saint, and getting on board the ship with the spoil, scoffed at the blessed man, and laughed him to scorn. But the Saint followed him even to the sea, and walking into the glassy seawaters up to the knees, with both hands lifted up to heaven he earnestly prays to Christ, who glorifies His chosen ones that glorify Him. Now that harbour, in which he stood and prayed to the Lord for some little while after the persecutor had sailed out, is in the place which in Scotic (Irish) is called Ait-Chambas Art-muirchol (Camus-an-Gaal, Ardnamurchan). Then in the next place the Saint, when he had finished his prayer and returned to the dry land, sits down in a more elevated place with his companions, to whom in that hour he utters these very terrible words, saying, 'This wretched creature, who hath despised Christ in His servants, will never return to the harbour from which he hath lately gone out in your presence; but neither will he arrive with his companions in evil-doing at other lands which he seeks, being prevented by sudden death. To-day will the fierce storm, which you will soon see arising out of a cloud on the north, be hurled against and drown him with his companions, nor will even one of them remain to tell the tale.' After waiting a very little while, on a most calm day, behold then the cloud rising from the sea, as the Saint had said, sent forth with mighty crash of wind, finding the robber with his spoil between the Malean and Colosan islands (Mull and Colonsay\ drowned him in the midst of the sea so suddenly lashed into fury; nor, according to the word of the Saint, did even one of those who had been in the ship escape; and in a wonderful manner, while on every side the whole of the sea remained calm, did such a single storm cast down to hell the robbers that were drowned miserably indeed, but deservedly.

Chapter Twenty-Three - Of One Feradach, Who Was Carried Off by Sudden Death

AT another time again, the holy man specially commended a certain exile of a noble family of the Picts, Tarain by name, committing him into the hand of one Feradach. a rich man, who dwelt -in the Ilean island (Islay), to live for some months in his retinue, as one of his friends. Whom when he had received, commended with such a commendation, from the hand of the holy man, after a few days, acting treacherously, he put to death by a cruel order. When this horrible wickedness was announced by some travellers to the Saint, he answered and spoke thus: 'That wretched creature, whose name will be blotted out of the book of life, hath not lied unto me, but unto God. These words we now speak in the middle of the summer season, but in the autumn, before he shall taste of swine's flesh fattened on the produce of trees, he will be carried off to the infernal regions, overtaken by sudden death.' This was the prophecy of the holy man; when he told it to the wretched creature, he despised and derided the Saint; and after some days of the autumn months, a sow fattened on the kernels of nuts is killed by his direction, other swine of the same man not yet being killed; he orders that the entrails be immediately taken out, and that a portion be quickly roasted for him on the spit, so impatient is the man to taste of it, and upset the prophecy of the blessed man. Which then being roasted, he asked for some small portion of a mouthful to be given him to taste, but before he could raise to his mouth the hand put forth to take it, he expired, and fell down dead on his back. Both they that saw and they that heard, greatly terrified and wondering, honoured and glorified Christ in His holy prophet.

Chapter Twenty-Four - Of a Certain Other Impious Man, a Persecutor of the Churches, Whose Name is called in Latin Manus Dextera

AT another time the blessed man, while staying in Hinba island (Eilean-na-Naoimh?), when he began to excommunicate some other persecutors of churches, namely, the sons of Conall son of Domhnall, one of whom was Ioan, of whom we have made mention above (Ch. 22), one of their companions in crime, by the instigation of the devil, rushed on with a spear to kill the Saint. To prevent which, one of the brethren, Findlugan by name, being ready to die for the holy man, came between, clad in his cowl. But in a wonderful manner such a garment of the blessed man, like some very strong and impenetrable armour, could not be pierced by the hard thrust of a very sharp spear by a man however strong, but remained unhurt, and he who was clothed in it was untouched and uninjured, protected by such a safeguard. But that accursed man, who was named Manus Dextera (Lamh-dess, right hand), went back, supposing that he had transfixed the holy man with his spear. A whole year afterwards from that day, when the Saint was living in the Iouan island (Iona), he says, 'Up to this day it is a full year from the day on which Lamhdess, so far as he could, killed Findlugan in my place; but he himself, as I think, is being slain in this hour.' Which, according to the revelation of the Saint, came to pass at the same moment in that island which may be called in Latin Longa (Luing), where Lamh-dess, himself alone, fell in some faction-fight between two parties, transfixed by the javelin of Cronan son of Baithene, hurled, as is reported, in the name of St. Columba; and after his death the men ceased to fight.

Chapter Twenty-Five - Of another Who Was a Persecutor of Innocents in Like Manner

WHEN the blessed man, as yet a young deacon, was living in the district of the Lagenians (Leinster) learning Divine wisdom, it happened one day that a certain man, a fierce, cruel persecutor of innocent persons, pursued a certain young girl as she fled on the level surface of the field. And when by chance she saw the old man Gemman, the tutor of the above-mentioned young deacon, reading in the field, she fled to him in a direct course, with all the speed she could. And he, alarmed by this sudden occurrence, calls to him

Columba, who is reading at a distance, that both of them, to the best of their power, may defend the girl from her pursuer. But he, immediately coming up, and showing no reverence to them, stabbed the girl under their cloaks with a lance, and, leaving her dead body lying over their feet, turned and began to go away. Then the old man, greatly distressed, turns to Columba and says, 'For how great length of time, O holy youth Columba, will God, the just judge, suffer this crime, with the dishonour to us, to be unavenged?' Then the Saint fitly pronounced this sentence upon the evil-doer himself, saying, 'In the same hour in which the soul of the girl slain by him ascends into the heavens, the soul of the murderer himself shall go down into hell.' And, sooner than can be said, with a word, like Ananias before Peter, so also that slaughterer of innocents, before the eyes of the holy youth, fell dead on that same spot of ground. The rumour of which sudden and dreadful vengeance was at once spread abroad through many districts of Scotia (Ireland), together with the wonderful fame of the holy deacon.

It may suffice to have spoken thus far of the terrible vengeances that fell on his adversaries. Now we will relate some few things concerning beasts.

Chapter Twenty-Six - Of a Boar Destroyed Through His Prayer

ANOTHER time, while the blessed man was staying some days in the Sci-an island (Skye) being alone, separated from the brethren a little further than usual in order to pray, he entered a thick wood and met a boar of won-drous size, which some hunting-hounds happened to be pursuing. And seeing him at a distance, the Saint stood still and looked at him. Then in the next place, calling on the Name of God, and raising his holy hand with earnest prayer, he says to him, 'Think not to come further this way; in the place to which thou hast now come, die!' And when this word of the Saint sounded through the woods, not only was that terrible wild beast unable to approach further, but quickly fell before his very face, struck dead by the power of his word.

Chapter Twenty-Seven - Of the Driving Away of a Certain Water Monster by the Virtue of the Prayer of the Blessed Man

AT another time again, when the blessed man was staying for some days in the province of the Picts, he found it necessary to cross the river Ness; and, when he came to the bank thereof, he sees some of the inhabitants burying a poor unfortunate little fellow, whom, as those who were burying him themselves reported, some water monster had a little before snatched at as he was swimming, and bitten with a most savage bite, and whose hapless corpse some men who came in a boat to give assistance, though too late, caught hold of by putting out hooks. The blessed man however, on hearing this, directs that some one of his companions shall swim out and bring to him the coble that is on the other bank, sailing it across. On hearing this direction of the holy and famous man, Lugne Mocumin, obeying without delay, throws off all his clothes except his under-garment, and casts himself into the water. Now the monster, which before was not so much satiated as made eager for prey, was lying hid in the bottom of the river; but perceiving that the water above was disturbed by him who was crossing, suddenly emerged, and, swimming to the man as he was crossing in the middle of the stream, rushed up with a great roar and open mouth. Then the blessed man looked on, while all who were there, as well the heathen as even the brethren, were stricken with very great terror; and. with his holy hand raised on high, he formed the saving sign of the cross in the empty air, invoked the Name of God, and commanded the fierce monster, saying, 'Think not to go further, nor touch thou the man. Quick! go back!' Then the beast, on hearing this voice of the Saint, was terrified and fled backward more rapidly than he came, as if dragged by cords, although before it had come so near to Lugne as he swam, that there was not more than the length of one punt-pole between the man and the beast. Then the brethren, seeing that the beast had gone away, and that their comrade Lugne was returned to them safe and sound in the boat, glorified God in the blessed man, greatly marvelling. Moreover also the barbarous heathens who were there present, constrained by the greatness of that miracle, which they themselves had seen, magnified the God of the Christians.

Chapter Twenty-Eight - Of the Land of This Island, Blessed by the Saint So That Thenceforth the Poisons of Vipers Should Hurt No Man Therein

ONE day of the same summer-time in which he departed to the Lord, the Saint goes, borne in a wagon, to visit the brethren who were engaged in heavy work in the western plain of the Iouan island (Iona). After some consolatory addresses spoken to them by the Saint, he, standing on a more elevated spot, thus prophesies, saying, 'From this day, my sons, I know that you will never for the future be able to see my face again in the places on this plain.' And seeing them greatly saddened on hearing this saying, and endeavouring to console them as much as might be, he lifts up both his holy hands, and, blessing the whole of this our island, says, l From this hour's space, the poisons of no vipers shall in any wise be able to hurt either men or cattle in the lands of this island, so long as the inhabitants of this same place of our sojourning observe the commands of Christ.

Chapter Twenty-Nine - Of a Knife blessed by the Saint with the Sign of the Lord's Cross

ANOTHER time, a brother named Molua, of the race of Briun, comes to the Saint, who at that same hour is writing, and says to him, 'Bless, I pray you, this knife which I have in my hand.' And he, stretching out his holy hand a little, blessed it, signing it with his pen, with his face turned to the book out of which he was writing. And as the abovementioned brother was going away with the knife that had been blessed, the Saint asks, saying, 'What knife have I blessed for a brother?' Diormit, his dutiful attendant, says, 'Thou hast blessed the knife used for killing bulls or oxen.' And he in reply answers and says, 'I trust in my Lord that the knife which I have blessed shall hurt neither man nor cattle.' Which word of the Saint was proved in that same hour to be most sure. For the same brother, going outside the fence of the monastery, and wishing to cut the throat of an ox, though he made three strong efforts, and with hard pushing too, yet he could not even pierce through the skin. The monks knowing this by experience, distributed the blade of the same knife by melting it in the heat of fire, and spreading it in a liquid state over all the iron instruments of the monastery; nor could they afterwards wound any flesh, the power of that benediction of the Saint abiding on them.

Chapter Thirty - Of the Healing of Diormit When Sick

AT another time, Diormit, the dutiful attendant of the Saint, was sick even unto death; the Saint came to visit him when placed in the last extremity; and, invoking the Name of Christ, standing at the bed of the sick man, and praying for him, said, 'Be Thou propitious unto me, I pray Thee, O my Lord, and take not away the soul of my dutiful attendant from the tabernacle of this flesh while I remain alive.' And having said this he remained silent for some little time. Then in the next place he utters this voice from his sacred mouth, saying, 'This my servant will not only not die this time, but will even live for many years after my decease.' And this, his supplication was heard, for Diormit, immediately after the effectual prayer of the Saint, recovered perfect health, and also survived for many years after the departure of the Saint to the Lord.

Chapter Thirty-One - Of the Healing of Fintan Son of Aedh When at the Point to Die

AT another time also, when the Saint was making a journey beyond the Dorsal Ridge of Britain (Drum-Alban), a certain youth, named Fintan, one of his companions, was distressed by sudden sickness, and brought almost to the last extremity, so his sorrowing comrades beseech the Saint to pray for him. He at once, having compassion on them, spreads out holy hands to heaven with earnest prayer, blesses the sick person, and says, 'This boy for whom you are pleading will enjoy a long life; and, after the death of us all who are here present, will remain alive, to die in a good old age.' Which prophecy of the blessed man was completely fulfilled throughout, for the same youth, afterwards the founder of the monastery called Kailli-au-inde (not identified), ended this present life in a good old age.

Chapter Thirty-Two - Of a Boy Whom the Venerable Man Brought to Life When Dead, in the Name of Christ the Lord

DURING that time in which St. Columba was staying for some days in the province of the Picts, a certain countryman with his whole household, when the holy man preached, hearing the word of life through an interpreter, believed; and, believing, was baptized, the husband with the wife and children and household servants. And, after some little interval of a few days, one of the sons of the father of the family, attacked by severe sickness, was brought almost to the border-lines between death and life. And when the Druids saw him dying, they began to mock at the parents with many reproaches, and to exalt their own gods as if stronger, but to detract from the God of the Christians as if weaker. And when all these things were reported to the blessed man, he is stirred up with zeal for God, and goes with his companions to the house of his friend the countryman, where the parents were performing the mournful funeral rites of their child lately deceased. The Saint, seeing them greatly distressed, encourages them and addresses them in consolatory words, that they may in no wise doubt of Divine omnipotence. And then he asks, saying, 'In what room does the body of the dead boy lie?' The bereaved father then leads the Saint under his saddened roof, and immediately, leaving the whole crowd shut away outside, he alone enters the sorrow-stricken dwelling, where there and then, on bended knees, copiously flooding his face with tears, he prays to Christ the Lord; and, rising after his kneeling, turns his eyes to the dead child, saying, 'In the Name of the Lord Jesus Christ, come to life, and stand upon thy feet.' With this glorious word of the Saint the soul returned to the body, and he that was dead revived with open eyes, and the apostolic man took his hand, raised him up, and steadied him in a standing posture; goes out of the house, taking him with him, and presented him alive again to his parents. Then the shouting of the people is raised on high, their mourning is turned into joy, the God of the Christians is glorified. Let our Columba then have as his own this miracle of power in common with Elijah and Elisha the prophets, and a like share of honour with Peter and Paul and John the apostles, in the raising of the dead; and among both companies, those namely of the prophets and of the apostles, may the prophetic and apostolic man have an honourable and eternal place in the heavenly country with Christ, Who liveth and reigneth with the Father, in the unity of the Holy Spirit, for ever and ever.

Chapter Thirty-Three - Of Broichan the Druid, Who was visited with Sickness for His Detention of a Maidservant, and Cured when she was Set Free

ABOUT the same time the venerable man requested of Broichan the Druid that a certain Scotic (Irish) female slave might be set at liberty, for pity's sake; and when he, by reason of his very hard and obstinate disposition, detained her, the Saint speaks to him and addresses him in this manner: 'Know, Broichan, know, that if thou wilt not deliver to me this captive stranger, thou wilt quickly die, even before I return from this province.' And, saying this in the presence of King Brude, he goes forth out of the royal dwelling, and comes to the river Ness, from which river he takes up a white stone, and says to his companions, 'Mark this white stone, by which the Lord will work many cures of the sick among this heathen people.' And having thus spoken, he next added a word, saying, 'Now is Broichan severely smitten, for an angel sent from heaven, heavily striking him, has shattered into many fragments the glass drinking-cup in his hand, from which he was drinking; and, moreover, has left him gasping feeble sighs, and nigh unto death. Let us wait a little in this place for two king's messengers, sent to us with all haste, that we may quickly assist the dying Broichan; now is Broichan terribly punished, ready to set the maiden free.' While the Saint is yet speaking these words, behold, as he predicted, there arrive two horsemen sent by the king, who declare all the things that have come to pass according to the prophecy of the Saint, in the case of Broichan, and in the fortress of the king, as to the breaking of the cup, the punishment of the Druid, and his being prepared to release the slave. And this, moreover, they added, saying, 'The king and his household have sent us to thee, that thou mayest assist his foster father Broichan, who is at the point of death.' Having heard these words of the messengers, the Saint sends to the king two out of the number of his companions, with the stone blessed by himself, saying, 'If in the first place Broichan will promise to set the maiden free, then let this little stone be put in water, and so let him drink of it, and straightway he will recover his health; but if he refuses, and resists the setting free of the slave, he shall immediately die.' The two messengers, obeying the word of the Saint, come to the royal hall, declaring to the king the words of the venerable man. On these being intimated to the king and his foster-father Broichan, they feared greatly, and the maidservant was set free in that same hour, and delivered to the messengers of the holy man. The stone is put in water, and in a wonderful manner, contrary to its nature, the pebble floats on the surface of the water like an apple or a nut, nor could the object blessed by the holy man be made to sink. Broichan, drinking from this floating stone, returned at once from approaching death, and recovered perfect health of body. So remarkable a stone, afterwards preserved among the king's treasures, in like manner put in water and swimming, effected, by the mercy of God, many cures of sicknesses among the people. Wonderful to relate, the same stone, though inquired for by these sick persons when their term of life had arrived, could never by any means be found. Thus also it was sought for on the day of the death of King Brude, yet it was not found in the same place where it had before been put away.

Chapter Thirty-Four - Of the Opposition of the Blessed Man against Broichan the Druid, and the Contrariety of the Wind

AFTER the above-mentioned events had taken place, Broichan one day addresses himself to the holy man and says, 'Tell me, Columba, what time dost thou propose to sail out?' 'On the third day,' says the Saint, 'if God will and I live, we propose to begin our voyage.' Broichan says in reply, 'Thou wilt not be able, for I can make the wind contrary for thee, and bring over thee a thick darkness.' The Saint says, 'The Almighty power of God ruleth over all things, and in His Name all our movements are directed, Himself being our governor.' Why more? As he had proposed in his heart, so the Saint came on the aforesaid day to the long lake of the river Ness, accompanied by a great following. But the Druids then began to rejoice when they saw a thick darkness come over, with a contrary wind and tempest. It is no marvel that, by God's permission, these things can sometimes be done by the artifice of demons, that even the winds and the seas are stirred up into a more stormy condition. For so at one time legions of demons met the holy bishop German in the midst of the sea, as he was sailing into Britain from the British Channel in the cause of human salvation, and stirred up storms that opposed their perils, covering the heaven and the day with the gloom of darkness. But at the prayer of German all these things ceased quicker than can be said; there came a calm, and the darkness was removed. Our Columba therefore, seeing the raging elements stirred against him, calls on Christ the Lord, and mounts the boat while the sailors are hesitating; he himself, with greater firmness, directs that the sail be hoisted up against the wind. Which being done, the whole multitude looking on, the craft flies along with amazing velocity, borne against adverse winds. And after no great space of time the contrary winds shift round to the help of the journey, and to the wonder of all. And so through all that day the boat of the blessed man was borne along by gentle and favourable breezes blowing, and landed at the desired haven. Let the reader therefore ponder well how great that venerable man was, and what manner of man, in whom Almighty God manifested His glorious Name in the sight of the heathen, by such miraculous powers as those above recorded.

Chapter Thirty-Five - Of the Sudden Opening of the Gate of the Royal Fortress of its Own Accord

AT another time, that is, just when the Saint was weary after his journey to King Brude, it happened by chance that the same king, lifted up by the royal pomp of his fortress, and bearing himself proudly, would not open the gates on the first arrival of the blessed man. As soon as the man of God knew it, he came with his companions to the folding-doors of the gateways, and, first making on them the sign of the Lord's cross, next he knocks, and lays his hand against the doors, which at once are opened of their own accord and with all speed, the bolts being driven back with great force. And as soon as they are open, the Saint next enters with his companions. On this being known, the king, with his council, in great alarm sets out from the house, and goes to meet the blessed man with all reverence, and very gently addresses him with conciliatory words. And from that day, and ever after, the same ruler held the holy and venerable man in very great honour, as was only right, all the remaining days of his life.

Chapter Thirty-Six - Of a Similar Unclosing of the Church of the Field of Two Rivers (Terryglass, Co. Tipperary)

ON another occasion again, the blessed man, staying for some days in Scotia (Ireland), went, on their invitation, to visit the brethren who were residing in the monastery of the Land of Two Rivers. But by some chance it so happened that, when he came to the church, the keys of the oratory could not be found. Now when the Saint heard the others inquiring among themselves about the locked doors and the keys not as yet found, he himself goes up to the door and says, 'The Lord is able to open His house for His servants without their keys.' With this saying, the bolts were then suddenly shot back with violent motion, and, the gate being open of its own accord, the Saint, amid the admiration of all, walks into the church before the rest, and, being hospitably received by the brethren, is venerated by all with great honour.

Chapter Thirty-Seven - Of a Certain Indigent Peasant for Whom the Saint Made a Stake for Killing Wild Animals, and Blessed It

AT another time, a certain very needy peasant came to the Saint, who was then living in the district which borders on the shores of the Aporic Lake (Lochaber). The blessed man, taking pity on this miserable person, who had not wherewith to feed his wife and children, gave him, when he begged, a certain alms, such as he could, and says, 'Poor fellow, take a stake from the neighbouring wood, and bring it to me quickly.' The miserable man obeyed, and, according to the direction of the Saint, brought the material, which the Saint took, and sharpened into a spear, and when he had brought it to a point with his own hand, he blessed it, and handed it to that poor man, and said, 'Carefully keep this spear, which, as I believe, will neither be able to hurt man nor any cattle, but only wild animals and also fishes; and so long as thou hast such a stake, there will never be wanting in thy house an abundant supply of deer's flesh.' The poor miserable mendicant on hearing this was greatly rejoiced, returned home, and fixed the spear in a secluded spot of the ground which wild animals frequented; and when the next night was past, first thing in the morning he goes in order to revisit the spear, and finds transfixed upon it a hart of wondrous size. Why more? No day could pass, so the tradition goes, in which he did not find that some hart or hind, or other animal, had fallen upon the, spear fixed in the ground. And, his whole house being thus filled with venison, he sold to his neighbours what he had to spare: that which the guest-room of his own house could not take in. But yet the envy of the devil found out this miserable man, as it did Adam, through his wife, who, not as a wise but as a foolish woman, thus spoke to her husband: 'Take the spear out of the ground; for if any men, or even cattle, die upon it, thou thyself and I also, with our children, shall either be slain or led captive.' To this the husband replies, 'It will not be so, for the holy man said to me as he blessed the stake, that it never would hurt men nor even cattle.' After these words the needy man, yielding to his wife, goes and takes the spear out of the ground, and senselessly put it in the house by the wall; soon his house-dog fell on it and died. And when the dog was gone, the wife again says, 'One of thy boys will fall on the stake and die.' On hearing her say this, he removes the spear from the wall and carries it back to the wood, and he fixed it among the thicker bushes, where, as he thought, it could be hit by no animal. But on his return the next day he found that a roe had fallen upon it and died. Removing it thence also, he fixed it in the river, which in Latin can be called Nigra Dea (not identified), hiding it under water near the bank, and revisiting it the next day, he found transfixed and retained on it a salmon of wondrous size, which, when he lifted it out of the river, he was scarcely able by himself to carry to the house, and, carrying the spear with him from the water at the same time, he fixed it outside in the upper part of the roof, and then a crow flew down and died on it, killed by the force of the swoop. Upon this the miserable man, misled by the counsel of his foolish wife, taking down the spear from the roof, took an axe, chopped it up into many little pieces, and cast them into the fire. And afterwards, having lost this effectual means of relieving his distress, he was again, as he deserved to be, reduced to beggary. This freedom from want, you see, depended on the stake so often mentioned above, which, so long as it was kept, could suffice for snares, and nets, and every kind of hunting and fishing, through the benediction of the blessed man. But when it was lost, the wretched peasant, though he had been enriched by it for the time, could only when too late, with the whole of his little household, lament over it all the rest of his days.

Chapter Thirty-Eight - Of the Milk-Bag which the Ebbing Tide Carried Away, and the Flowing Tide Restored in the Place Where it was before

AT another time, the messenger of the blessed man, named Lugaid, sur-named Lathir, was at his command proposing to sail to Scotia (Ireland); and, finding among the sailing appliances of the Saint's ship a milk-bag that he was looking for, he put it to soak in the sea, piling some good-sized stones over it, and, coming to the Saint, told him what he had done with the bag. Who smilingly says, 'I think that the bag, which thou sayest thou hast put un-der the waves, will not go with thee to Ireland this time.' 'Why,' says he, 'shall I not be able to have it with me in the ship?' 'Another day,' says the Saint, 'thou wilt know what the event will prove.' And so Lugaid goes on the morn-ing of the next day to bring back his bag from the sea; the ebbing tide had however carried it away during the night. And on its not being found, he re-turned in sadness to the Saint, threw himself on the ground on bended knees, and confessed his negligence. Then the Saint consoled him, saying, 'Brother, do not grieve over perishable things; the bag which the ebbing tide has taken away, the flowing tide will bring back to its own place after thy departure.' The same day, after Lugaid had set out from the Iouan island (Iona), the of-fice of the ninth hour having been said, the Saint thus addresses those who are standing about, and says, 'Now let one of you go to the sea; the flowing tide has now brought back the bag about which Lugaid was lamenting, and which the ebbing tide had carried away, and has put it back in the place whence it was removed.' On hearing this saying of the Saint, a certain active youth ran down to the water's edge, and, finding the bag, as the Saint had predicted, returned and brought it back, running in his excitement, greatly delighted, and laid it before the Saint, to the admiration of all who were there present.

In these two narratives above written, although in small matters, the stake, namely, and the bag, prophecy and a miracle of power, as has often been said, are perceived to accompany one another.

Now let us pass on to other matters.

Chapter Thirty-Nine - A Prophecy of the Holy Man Regarding Libran of the Reed-Ground

AT another time, while the holy man was living in the Iouan island (Iona), a certain countryman who had lately taken the clerical habit, sailing over from Scotia (Ireland), came to the island monastery of the blessed man. And one day, when the Saint found him sitting alone in the guesthouse, and on his being first questioned by the Saint as to his country, his family, and the cause of his journey, he stated that he was born in the region of the Connachtae (Connaught), and had wearied himself by a long journey in order to wipe out his sins in a pilgrimage. And when the Saint, in order to make trial of the quality of his penitence, put before his eyes the hard and laborious monastic regulations, he at once makes answer to the Saint, and says, 'I am prepared to do all things whatsoever thou wilt bid me, however hard, however humiliating.' Why say more? That same hour he confessed all his sins, and promised, on his knees bent to the ground, that he would fulfil the penitential canons. The Saint says to him, 'Rise, and be seated.' Then, while he is sitting, he thus addresses him: 'Seven years' penance must thou fulfil in the Ethican land (Tiree). Thou and I, God granting it, are to live until thou completest the number of seven years.' Comforted by these words of the Saint, and giving thanks to God, he says to the Saint, 'What ought I to do as to a particular false oath that I have taken? For I killed a certain poor fellow while staying in my native land, and after his murder I was kept in bonds as the guilty person. But a man who was related to me, of the same parentage, and greatly abounding in riches, came to the rescue, and was just in time to loose me from my bonds when bound, and he so delivered me when condemned to die. And, after my release, I promised, swearing solemnly, that I would serve him all the days of my life. But after some days spent in servitude, disdaining the service of man, and desiring rather to obey God, I got away, a deserter from that earthly master, thus breaking my oath, and I have now come to thee, the Lord prospering my journey.' To this the Saint, seeing that the man is very greatly troubled about such matters, prophesying as before, makes answer, saying, 'After the completion of seven years, as has been told thee, thou shalt come hither to me for the forty days of Lent, that in the Paschal festival thou mayest go up to the altar, and receive the Eucharist.' Why linger we over words? The penitent pilgrim obeys in all respects the commands of the holy man. And having been sent in those days to the monastery of the Plain of Lunge (in Tiree), and his se\en years being fully completed there in penance, he returns to the Saint in the days of Lent, according to his former prophetic bidding. And after the completion of the Paschal solemnity, in which he went up to the altar as bidden, he came to the Saint, asking him about the above-mentioned oath. To whom, when he asks such things, the Saint makes answer, prophesying, 'Thine earthly master, of whom thou formerly spakest to me, is still alive, and thy father and mother and brethren yet live. Now therefore thou oughtest to prepare thyself to sail.' And while thus speaking he offered to him a sword ornamented with carved tusks of beasts, saying, 'Accept this gift to take with thee, and offer it to the master for thy ransom, but yet he will in no wise accept it. For he has a wife who is well disposed, to whose wholesome counsel he will defer, and the same day he will present thee with thy freedom without money and without price, loosing from thy loins the usual captive's girdle. But though relieved from this anxiety, thou wilt not escape another disquietude arising beside it; for thy brethren will press thee on every side to make good the support due to thy father for so long a time, yet neglected. But do thou, without any hesitation, fall in with their desire, and receive thine aged father to be dutifully cherished. And there is no need for thee to be distressed about this burden, however weighty it may seem to thee, for soon thou wilt lay it down; for from whatsoever day thou beginnest to attend to thy father, on another day in the end of the same week thou wilt bury his dead body. But after the burial of thy father thy brethren will again keenly set upon thee to render the same offices of piety, due also to thy mother. Thy younger brother however will free thee from that obligation, for he, being ready in thy place, will render for thee to thy mother, as her attendant, every work of filial duty.'

After these words, the above-named brother. Libran by name, accepted the gift and went on his way, enriched by the benediction of the Saint; and, on coming to his native land, he found all things proved to be true, according to the prophecy of the Saint. For as soon as he showed the price of his freedom, offering it to his master, the wife, remonstrating with him for being willing to accept it, says, 'Why should we accept this price which holy Columba has sent? Of this we are not worthy. Let this dutiful servant be delivered to him without payment. The blessing of the holy man will profit us more than this price which is offered.' And so the husband, on hearing this wholesome counsel of the wife, at once set the servant free without payment. And he afterwards, according to the prophecy of the Saint, being compelled by his brethren, began to minister to his father, and buried him when dead, on the seventh day. And when his father is buried, he is compelled to render due service to his mother. But, a younger brother coming to the rescue, as the Saint had predicted, and supplying his place, he is released. And this brother thus spake to the other brethren: 'We ought by no means to detain our brother at home, now that he has worked out the salvation of his soul for seven years with holy Columba in Britain.'

After which, released from all the matters by which he was troubled, and bidding farewell to his mother and brothers, he returned a free man, and came to the place which in Scotic (Irish) is called Daire Calgaich (Derry); and finding there a ship under sail setting out from the harbour, he calls from the shore and eagerly begs that the mariners will take him with them to sail to Britain. But they would not receive him, and bade him begone; because they were not monks of St. Columba. Then in the next place, speaking to that same venerable man, although absent so far away, yet present in spirit, as the event soon proved, he says, 'Doth it please thee, O holy Columba, that these mariners, who will not take me who am thy companion, should sail out with full sails and prosperous winds?' While he said this, the wind, which before was favourable for them, quicker than it can be told, veered round and was contrary. Meanwhile, seeing the same man running in a line with them by the side of the river, the sailors all on a sudden take counsel among themselves, and say, calling out to him from the ship, 'Perhaps it is on this account that the wind so quickly veered round to the direction contrary for us, because we refused to take thee with us. But if even now we invite thee to us into the ship, wilt thou be able to change the winds that are now contrary for us into favouring breezes?' Hearing these words, the traveller said to them, 'The holy Columba, to whom I am going, and whom I have served thus far for seven years, can obtain a fair wind for you from his Lord, by virtue of his prayers, if ye will take me.' On hearing this, they draw the ship up to the land, and invite him to come into it to them. And he at once, having mounted into the ship, says, 'In the name of the Almighty, whom the holy Columba blamelessly serves, haul up your sail with tightened cordage.' Which being done, the contrary gales of wind are at once turned into favouring breezes, and there succeeded a prosperous voyage into Britain under full sails. And Libran, after they had arrived on British shores, left that ship, blessed the sailors, and came to St. Columba, then dwelling in the Iouan island (Iona). Which blessed man, mark you, joyfully received him, and fully declared to him all the things that had taken place in connexion with him by the way, no other person giving any intimation; about his master, and his wife's wholesome counsel, how by her persuasion he was set free; also about his brothers, and the death of his father, and the burial at the end of the week, about his mother, and the seasonable help of the younger brother; about those things that occurred on his return journey, the wind being contrary, and then favourable; about the words of the sailors who at first refused to take him, about the promise of a favouring wind, and the favourable change of the wind when he was received into the ship. Why say more? Everything which the Saint had before prophesied as to be fulfilled, he then related as having been fulfilled.

After these words the traveller returned the price of his ransom which he had received from the Saint. To him the Saint in the same hour assigned a name, saying. 'Thou shalt be called Libran because thou art free' (*liber*). Which Libran, mark you, in those same days, faithfully took the monastic vow. And when he was being sent back by the holy man to the monastery in which he previously for seven years served the Lord as a penitent, he received from him as he bade him farewell these prophetic words, uttered concerning himself: 'Thou shalt live a long life, and close the present life in a good old age. Not, however, in Britain, but in Scotia (Ireland), will thy resurrection be.' Hearing this word, he wept bitterly, on bended knees. And the Saint, seeing him much distressed, began to console him, saying, 'Arise, and let not thine heart be troubled. Thou shalt die in one of mine own monasteries, and with my chosen monks in the kingdom shall thy portion be; with them shalt thou awake from the sleep of death to the resurrection of life.' He then, having received from the Saint no ordinary consolation, greatly rejoiced, and, made rich by the benediction of the Saint, went on his way in peace. Which true prophecy of the Saint concerning the same man was afterwards fulfilled. For, while he served the Lord in obedience in the monastery of the Plain of Lunge, through many rolling years after the passing away of St. Columba from the world, the monk, being sent in extreme old age to Scotia (Ireland) on some monastic service, as soon as he went down from the ship, passed through the Plain of Breg (in Meath) and came to the monastery of Oak Plain (Durrow); and there, received as a guest in the guest-house, afflicted by some infirmity, on the seventh day of his sickness, he departed in peace to the Lord, and was buried among the chosen monks of St. Columba, according to his prophecy, to rise to eternal life. Let it suffice to have written these truthful prophecies of St. Columba concerning Libran of the Reedground. Which Libran, mark you, is so called 'Of the Reed-ground,' because for many years he had laboured in a reed-ground, getting reeds.

Chapter Forty - Of a Certain Poor Woman Who, as a Daughter of Eve, Suffered Great and Very Difficult Pains of Childbirth

ONE day, while the Saint is living in the Iouan island (Iona), he rises from his reading, and says, smiling, 'Now I must hasten to the oratory, that I may beseech the Lord for a certain poor afflicted woman, who is now in Ireland, and in her cries is calling on the name of this Columba, being tortured in strong pains of most difficult child-birth, and so hopes that, through me, release from her sufferings will be given her by the Lord, because she is related to me, having a father sprung from the family of my mother.' Thus speaking, the Saint, moved with compassion for that poor woman, runs to the church, and on bended knees prays for her to Christ Who was born of mankind. And, having gone out of the oratory after prayer, he speaks to the brethren who meet him, saying, 'Now is the Lord Jesus merciful. He Who was born of a woman, seasonably helping an afflicted woman, has delivered her from her pains, and she has safely borne a child, nor will she die this time.' The same hour, as the Saint prophesied, the poor afflicted woman, calling on his name, was released, and recovered her health. So it was afterwards stated by certain persons who came over from Scotia (Ireland), and from the same district where the woman dwelt.

Chapter Forty-One - Of One Lugne, a Pilot, Surnamed Tudida, Whom, as Being Ill-Favoured, His Wife Disliked, and who Lived in the Rechrean Island (Rathlin, or Lambay?)

AT another time, while the Saint was being entertained in the Rechrean island, a certain countryman came to him and complained about his wife, who, as he said, had taken a dislike to him, and would in no wise allow him to come near her for marriage rights. On hearing this, the Saint called the wife to him, and, so far as he could, began to reprove her on that account, saying, 'Wherefore, woman, dost thou endeavour to repel from thee thine own flesh, when the Lord saith, "They twain shall be in one flesh"? Therefore the flesh of thy husband is thine own flesh.' She answers and says, 'All things whatsoever thou shalt enjoin to me, though they be ever so severe, I am prepared to fulfil, one thing only excepted, that in no wise thou constrain me to sleep in one bed with Lugne. I do not refuse to undertake all the management of the house; or, if thou biddest, even to cross the seas, and remain in some monastery of maidens.' The Saint then says, 'That which thou sayest cannot be rightly done, for thou art bound by the law of a husband so long as the husband liveth. For it would be a sin for those whom God hath lawfully joined to be put asunder.' And, having thus spoken, he next added, 'In this day three persons, that is, I and the husband, with the wife, will pray unto the Lord, fasting.' Hereupon she says, 'I know that to thee it will not be impossible that those things which appear to be difficult, or even impossible, may be granted, when sought of God.' Why say more? The wife the same day agrees to fast with the Saint, and the husband likewise; the following night the Saint prayed for them, taking no sleep; and on the next day the Saint, in the husband's presence, thus addresses the wife: 'O woman, art thou prepared to-day, as thou wast saying yesterday, to go out to a monastery of women?' She says, 'Now I know that thy prayer concerning me is heard by God, for the man whom yesterday I disliked today I love; for during this last night my heart, how I know not, has been changed in me from dislike to love.' Why make a long story? From that same day to the day of her death the soul of this wife was indissolubly cemented in love of her husband, so that in no way did she thenceforth deny those rights of marriage which before she refused to render.

Chapter Forty-Two - A Prophecy of the Blessed Man Concerning the Voyage of Cormac, a Descendant of Lethan

AT another time Cormac, a soldier of Christ, about whom we have briefly recorded some few things in the first book of this little work (Book One, Ch. Six), tried even a second time to look for a desert in the sea. And after he had gone out from the land with full sails through the boundless ocean, in those days St. Columba, while staying beyond the Ridge of Britain (Drum-Alban), commended him to King Brude in the presence of the sub-king of the Orcades (Orkneys), saying, 'Some of our men have lately gone out, desiring to find a desert in the boundless sea, and, in case they should after long circuits arrive at the Orcades, do thou now earnestly commend them to this sub-king, who has hostages in thy hand, lest any misfortune should happen to them while they are within the bounds of his kingdom.' Now the Saint thus pleaded with regard to this thing, because in spirit he knew beforehand that after some months the same Cormac would be coming to the Orcades. Which afterwards so came to pass; and, through the above-mentioned commendation of the holy man, he was delivered from impending death while in the Orcades. After a moderate interval of a few months, while the Saint was living in the Iouan island (Iona), one day there arises unexpectedly in his presence a mention of the same Cormac, made by some persons engaged in conversation and speaking to this effect: 'How Cormac's voyage is progressing, whether it be prosperous or not, is as yet unknown.' Which remark being heard by the Saint, he speaks on this wise, saying, 'You will be seeing Cormac, of whom you are now speaking, arriving here presently to-day.' And after the space of about one hour, wonderful to relate, behold! Cormac, arriving so unexpectedly, walks into the oratory amid the admiration and thanksgivings of all.

And now, seeing that we have briefly introduced the prophesying of the blessed man concerning the second voyage of this man Cormac, we must also write some account of his equally prophetic knowledge concerning the third voyage.

When the same Cormac was toiling over the ocean wave for a third time, he began to be imperiled, well-nigh unto death. For when his ship ran out from the land under full sails in a direct course, even to the region of the northern sky, the south wind blowing for fourteen days and as many nights of the summer season, such navigation seemed to be beyond the limit of human wandering, and return impossible. Whence it came to pass, that after the tenth hour of that same fourteenth day, some terrors almost too great to be borne, and indeed very formidable, arose together on every side; certain foul and very dangerous creatures, which indeed up to that time had not been seen, swarmed around, covering the sea; and with horrible violence struck bottom and sides, stern and prow, with such heavy blows, that it was thought they might go through the ship's covering of hides. And, as those there present afterwards stated, they were about the size of frogs, very formidable, being furnished with stings; they were not flying, but swimming creatures, yet they also attacked the blades of the oars. On seeing these, among other monsters, of which time forbids us now to tell, Cormac and the sailors who accompanied him are greatly troubled and much afraid, and with many tears pray to God, Who is a very present help in trouble. The same hour also our own St. Columba, although far absent in body, yet was present in spirit in the ship with Cormac. Wherefore, at the same moment he rings his bell and calls the brethren to the oratory; and on entering the church, he prophesies and speaks to them in the manner usual with him, as they stand around, saying, 'Brethren, pray ye with all earnestness for Cormac, who has now sailed beyond the limit of human voyaging, taking an unbounded course, and is at present enduring some horrible terrors, never before experienced, and almost indescribable, caused by sea-monsters. Therefore ought we in heart to compassionate our fellow-members and brethren now placed in peril past all endurance, and supplicate the Lord with them. For, behold! now Cormac, with his sailors, copiously flooding his face with tears, is earnestly praying to Christ; let us also help our brother by praying that Christ will have mercy on us, and change into the north that south wind which has now been blowing these fourteen days; that this north wind, you see, may bring Cormac's ship out of these perils.' And, thus speaking, in a plaintive voice, and on bended knees before the altar, he supplicates the Almighty power of God, which governs the winds and waves and all things else. And after his prayer he quickly rises, wipes his tears, and joyfully gives thanks to God, saying, 'Now, brethren, let us rejoice with our dear ones for whom we pray, for the Lord will now change the south wind into a north wind, which will bring our fellow members out of their perils, and bear them back to us again.' And immediately, even as he spoke, the south wind ceased, and a north wind blew for many days after, and Cormac's ship was brought back to land. And Cormac came to St. Columba, and, God granting it, they beheld each other face to face, to the great admiration and no ordinary joy of all.

Let the reader therefore weigh well how great, and of what spirit, the blessed man was, that he had such prophetic knowledge, and, by invoking the Name of Christ, could command the winds and the sea.

Chapter Forty-Three - Of the Journey of the Venerable Man in a Car, without the Security of the Car's Linch-Pins

AT another time, while the Saint was staying for some days in Scotia (Ireland), compelled by some ecclesiastical engagements, he mounts a yoked car that had previously been blessed by him; but, from some negligence that occurred, what it was is not known, the necessary linch-pins had not first been put through the holes at the ends of the axles. Now on, the same occasion it was Columban son of Eochaid, a holy man, founder of that monastery which in the Scotic (Irish) tongue is called Snamluthir (Slanore), who rendered the service of driver in the same car with St. Columba. Therefore there was on that day such a jolting over long stretches of roads, without any separation or loosening of the wheels and the shoulders of the axles; and, as has been said above, without any retention or security of linch-pins holding them on. But it was by Divine grace alone so granting it to the venerable man, that the car in which he was safely seated went on in a direct course without any hindrance.

Thus far it may suffice to have written of the miracles of power, which Divine omnipotence wrought through the famous man while having his portion in this present life. Now also there are some few to be put on record, of those which are proved to have been granted to him by the Lord after his passing away from the body.

Chapter Forty-Four - Of Rain Poured Out Over the Thirsting Land after Some Months of Drought, the Lord Granting it for the Honour of the Blessed Man

FOR, indeed, about fourteen years ago, there happened in these barren lands in the spring-time a very great drought, continuous and severe, insomuch that the threatening of the Lord applied in the Book of Leviticus to the people who were transgressors appeared to be hanging over us, where He says, 'I will make for you the heaven above as iron, and the earth brass. Your labour shall be spent in vain; the earth shall not bring forth her bud, nor the trees yield fruit,' &c. We therefore, reading these words, and dreading a plague hanging over us, took counsel and agreed that this should be done, namely, that some of our seniors should walk round the newly ploughed and sown field, with the white tunic of St. Columba, and with books written with his own pen; and that they should lift up in the air, and shake out three times, the same tunic in which he was clothed in the hour of his departure from the flesh; and open his books, and read them on the Angels' hill (Sithean Mor), where sometimes the citizens of the heavenly country have been seen to descend to an interview with the blessed man (Book Three, Ch. 16). After all these things had been done according to the counsel taken, wonderful to say, on that same day, the sky, bare of clouds during the past months, March, to wit, and April, was with wonderful rapidity overspread with them, as they ascended from the sea in that place, and there came a great rain, falling day and night; and the earth, before so thirsty, but now thoroughly saturated, produced its shoots in due season, and, in the same year, very joyful cornfields. And thus the mention of the name alone of the blessed man being called to mind, in the tunic and in the books, profited at the same time many places and peoples both serviceably and seasonably.

Chapter Forty-Five - Of Contrary Gales of Wind Changed into Favourable Breezes by the Power of the Prayers of the Venerable Man

THE present miracles that we ourselves have seen, undoubtedly confirm our belief in those of past time, which we have not seen. For we ourselves have thrice seen contrary gales of wind made favourable. The first time was when some long dug-out boats of pine and oak were drawn over the land, and great timbers both for ships and for houses were carried out; we took counsel, and placed on the altar, with psalms and fasting, and invocation of his name, the vestures and books of the blessed man, that he might obtain from the Lord fair winds for our benefit. Which so came to pass, God granting it to the same holy man, for in that day in which our sailors, all preparations being made, proposed to tow through the sea with their boats and coracles the timbers of the above-mentioned materials, the winds, contrary in the previous days, were suddenly changed in our favour. Then in the next place, God being propitious, favouring breezes serving them the whole day, and with full sails, without any hindrance, all that naval expedition prosperously came through long and indirect channels to the Iouan island (Iona).

But a second time, when, after the lapse of some years, some other oak timbers, together with ourselves, were being towed from the mouth of the river Sale (the Seil in Lorne?) for the repairs of our monastery, and, twelve coracles having been got together, on one calm day, while the sailors were sweeping the sea with their oars, suddenly arises against us a west wind, also called the Zephyr, and we then turn aside for the nearest island, which in Scotic (Irish) is called Airthrago (Kerrera?), seeking therein a harbour of refuge. But meanwhile we complain of that inconvenient contrary state of the wind, and we begin somehow as it were to accuse our Columba, saying, 'Doth this our unfortunate detention please thee, O Saint? Hitherto we have hoped that thou wouldst grant us, God being propitious, some comforting help in our labours, reckoning thee, indeed, to be a man of some great honour in the sight of God.' When we had thus spoken, after a little space, as it were of a single moment, wonderful to say, behold , the contrary west wind ceases, and, more quickly than can be said, a favourable south-east wind blows. The sailors, receiving their orders, then haul up the yards in the form of a cross, and also the sails, with extended ropes, and, reaching our island the same day with favouring and gentle breezes, we are conveyed without any laborious work, together with all the fellow-workers in our boats, rejoicing in the conveyance of the timbers. That querulous accusation of the holy man, slight as it was, profited us not a little. And of how great and of what manner of merit in the sight of the Lord is the Saint whom He Himself had heard, appears in so rapid a change of the winds.

Then a third time was, when during the summer season, after the meeting of an Irish synod, we were detained for some days by contrary winds among the people of the tribe of Lorne, and reached the Sainean island (Shuna), and there the festival eve, and solemn day of St. Columba, found us waiting, and very sad, being desirous, you see, to keep it as a joyful day in the Iouan island (Iona). Wherefore, as on another former occasion, we complained, saying, 'Doth it please thee, O Saint, that we should spend to-morrow, the day of thy festival, among country-folk, and not in thy church? It is an easy thing for thee in the beginning of such a day to obtain from the Lord that contrary winds be changed into favourable, and that we celebrate in thy church the solemnities of the masses of thy birthday' (festival). After passing that night, we rise early in the morning, and, seeing that the contrary winds have ceased, we mount our ships with no wind blowing, and advance into the sea; when, behold, immediately the south wind, also called Notus, blows after us. Then the sailors joyously run up the sails, and so on that day, God granting it to the blessed man, our voyage was such, without labour, so rapid, and so prosperous, that, as we before desired, arriving at the harbour of the Iouan island after the third hour of the day (9 a.m.), the washing of hands and feet being finished after that, we entered the church with the brethren at the sixth hour (noon), and celebrated together the sacred solemnities of masses, on the feast day, I say, of the birth (into the future life) of St. Columba and St. Baithene (June 9); in the dawning of which day, as has been said above, we set out from the Sainean island, situated at a great distance. Now there are yet living witnesses of this story above related, and not only two or three, according to the law, but one hundred arid more.

Chapter Forty-Six - Of the Plague

AND this also, as I think, appears to be something not to be reckoned among the smaller miracles of power, namely, concerning the plague which in our times has twice laid waste the world in its greater part. For, not to mention other wider regions of Europe, namely, Italy and the Roman city itself, and the Cisalpine provinces of the Gauls, also those of Spain, separated by the barrier of the Pyrenean mountain range; the isles of the sea throughout, Scotia (Ireland) and Britain for instance, have on two occasions been wasted by dreadful pestilence; except two races, that is to say, the people of the Picts, and that of the Scots (Irish colonists) of Britain, between whom the hills of the Britannic ridge (Drum-Alban) form a boundary. And, although there are not wanting great sins of both tribes, sins by which the eternal Judge is generally provoked to anger, yet He has spared both thus far, bearing patiently with them. Now to what other person is this grace, granted them by God, attributed, but to St. Columba, whose monasteries, founded within the boundaries of both peoples, have been held in very great honour by both, up to the present time? Yet this which we are now about to say is not to be heard, we think, without a sigh, that there are many in both races very senseless, who, not knowing that they are defended from diseases by the prayers of the Saints, and being unthankful, wickedly abuse the patience of God. But we render frequent thanks to God, Who defends us also from the assaults of pestilences in these our islands, while our venerable patron prays for us; and in Saxonia (England), when we visited my friend King Aldfrid while the plague had not yet ceased, and was wasting many villages here and there, yet both in its first onset after the war of Ecfrid, and in a second, two years having intervened, the Lord so delivered us while walking in such danger in the midst of mortality, that not even one of our companions died, nor was any one of them troubled by any disease.

This second book, of Miracles of power, must now be ended, and in it the reader ought to take notice that even of those which are well ascertained, many have been omitted in order not to fatigue our readers.

Here Beginneth the Third Book, of Angelic Visitations

Preface

IN the first of these three books, as has been mentioned above, we have described briefly and succinctly, the Lord helping us, some of the Prophetic revelations. In the second and preceding book, some of the Miracles of power which have been shown through the blessed man, and which, as has often been said, the grace of prophecy for the most part accompanies. But in this third book, some of the Angelic apparitions which have been revealed either to others concerning the blessed man, or to himself concerning others; and of these, some which have been manifested to both parties, although in different measure, that is, to himself specially and more fully, but to others not specially, and only in part, that is, externally and tentatively, yet in the same visions, whether of angels or of celestial light. Whatever in any case may be the discrepancies in such visions, they will be resolved where they are written below in their places. But now, to begin our description of the angelic apparitions from the earliest origins of the birth of the blessed man.

Chapter One - Of the Angel of the Lord who Appeared to His Mother in Dreams after His Conception in the Womb

ONE night, between the conception and birth of the venerable man, the angel of the Lord appeared in dreams to his mother, and let down to her, as he stood by her, a certain robe of wondrous beauty, in which the beautiful colours as it were of all flowers appeared to be depicted, and which after some short interval he asked to have back, and took it from her hands, and, lifting it up and spreading it out, let it go in the empty air. But she, being made sad by its being taken away from her, so speaks to that man of worshipful presence, 'Why dost thou so soon take away from me this delightful mantle?' He immediately replies, 'For this reason, because this cloak belongs to some one of such distinguished honour, that thou wilt not be able to keep it longer with thee.' After these words, the woman saw the above-mentioned mantle gradually lengthening from her in its flight, and increasing in size so as to exceed the breadth of the plains, and to overtop the mountains and woods in its greater measure, and she heard a voice following thus: 'Woman, be not sad, for to the man to whom thou art joined in the marriage compact thou shalt bear so famous a son, that he will be numbered with the prophets of God as one of themselves, predestinated by God as the leader of innumerable souls to the celestial country.' And while she is hearing this voice the woman awakes.

Chapter Two - Of a Luminous Ray Seen Over the Face of the Boy Himself As He Slept

ON another night, the presbyter Cruithnechan, a man of admirable life, the foster-father of the same blessed boy, returning after mass from the church to his dwelling, found the whole of his house irradiated by a bright light. He saw, in fact, a globe of fire standing over the face of the sleeping child; at the sight of which he immediately quaked with fear, and, falling down with his face to the earth, greatly wondering, he understood that the grace of the Holy Spirit was poured out from heaven upon his foster-child.

Chapter Three - Of an Apparition of Holy Angels whom St. Brendan Saw in Company with the Blessed Man, Walking With Him through the Field

FOR, after the space of many seasons, when St. Columba was excommunicated by a certain synod for some venial and, so far, excusable matters, not rightly, as afterwards became clear at the last, he came to the same assembly that had been gathered against himself. And when St. Brendan, the founder of that monastery which in Scotic (Irish) is called Birra (of Birr), while at a distance, saw him approaching, he quickly rises, and with face bowed down, reverently kisses him. When some seniors in that assembly, the rest being placed apart, were finding fault with him, saying, 'Why dost thou not decline to rise before, and to kiss, an excommunicated person?' he speaks to them on this wise, and says, 'If ye had seen what the Lord hath not disdained to show to me this day with regard to this His chosen one, whom ye dishonour, ye would never have excommunicated one, whom, not only doth God in no wise excommunicate in accordance with your improper sentence, but even more and more exalteth.' They on the other side say, 'How, we should like to know, doth God, as thou sayest, glorify him whom we have excommunicated, and not without cause?' 'I have seen,' says Brendan, 'a very luminous column of fiery hair going before the man of God whom ye despise, and also holy angels, the companions of his walk through the field. Therefore I dare not slight this man, whom I see to be foreordained by God to be the leader of the peoples unto life.' When he had thus spoken, not only did they desist, not daring to go further in excommunicating the Saint, but they even honoured him with great veneration. This thing was done in Teilte (Teltown).

Chapter Four - Of the Angel of the Lord Whom St. Finnian Saw as the Companion of the Blessed Man's Journey

AT another time, the holy man visited the venerable bishop Finnian, his former master; that is to say, the young man visited the old man. And when St. Finnian saw him approaching towards him, he saw at the same time an angel of the Lord, the companion of his journey; and, as is handed down to us by well-informed persons, he mentioned it to certain brethren standing by, saying. 'Behold! now ye may see approaching us the holy Columba, who has merited to have an angel from heaven as the companion of his journey.'

In those days the Saint sailed over to Britain with twelve comrades, his disciples.

Chapter Five - Of the Angel of the Lord who appeared visibly to St. Columba While Staying in Hinba Island, when sent to Ordain Aedhan to Be King

AT another time, while the famous man was staying in Hinba island (Eile-an-na-Naoimh?), one night in an ecstasy of mind he saw an angel of the Lord sent to him, who had in his hand the glassy book of the ordination of kings, which the venerable man, when he had received it from the hand of the angel, at his bidding began to read. And when he refused to ordain Aedhan to be king, as was recommended to him in the book, because he loved logenan his brother more; suddenly the angel put out his hand and smote the Saint with a scourge, the livid mark of which remained on his side all the days of his life. And he added this word, saying, 'Know for certain that I am sent unto thee from God with the glassy book, that, according to the words which thou hast read in it, thou mayest ordain Aedhan to the kingdom. And if thou art not willing to obey this command, I will smite thee again.' When, therefore, this angel of the Lord appeared for three nights in succession, having in his hand that glassy book, and committed to him the same commands of the Lord concerning the ordination of that king, the Saint, obeying the word of the Lord, sailed over to the Iouan island (Iona), and there ordained Aedhan, who arrived in those days, to be king, as he had been commanded. And among the words of ordination he prophesied future events concerning his sons and grandsons and great grandsons, and, placing his hand upon his head, ordained and blessed him.

Cuimine (Cummian) the Fair, in the book which he wrote of the virtues of St. Columba, has thus said, that St. Columba began to prophesy of Aedhan and his posterity, and of his kingdom, saying, 'Believe without doubting, Aedhan, that none of thine adversaries will be able to resist thee, until thou first actest fraudulently against me and against my successors. Wherefore, then, do thou commend it to thy sons, that they may commend it to their sons and grandsons and posterity, lest they through evil counsels lose the sceptre of this their kingdom out of their hands. For at whatsoever time they do anything against me or against my kinsmen who are in Ireland, the scourge, which for thy sake I have endured from the angel, shall by the hand of God be turned upon them to their great disgrace, and the heart of men shall be taken away from them, and their enemies shall be greatly strengthened over them.'

Now this prophecy has been fulfilled in our own times, in the battle of Roth (Magh Rath, fought 637), when Domhnall Brecc, grandson of Aedhan, without cause wasted the province of Domhnall, grandson of Ainmire. And from that day to this they are ever on the decline through means of strangers, which excites in the breast deep sighs of grief.

Chapter Six - Of an Apparition of Angels Carrying to Heaven the Soul of a Certain Blessed Brito

AT another time, while the holy man was staying in the Iouan island (Iona), one of his monks, Brito, intent on good deeds, being seized with bodily sickness, was brought to the last extremity. When the venerable man visited him in the hour of his departure, standing a little while by his bed, and blessing him, he quickly goes out home, unwilling to see him dying. And he, in the very moment after the holy man had left the house, closed this present life. Then the famous man, walking in the courtyard of his monastery with his eyes lifted up to heaven, was for some time lost in amazement, greatly wondering. But a certain brother, Aedhan by name, son of Libir, a religious man and one of a good disposition, the only one of the brethren who was present at that hour, on bended knees began to ask the Saint to tell him the reason for such great astonishment. To whom the Saint replies, 'Now have I seen in the air holy angels warring against hostile powers, and I give thanks to Christ, the Witness of the conflict, that the victorious angels have carried up to the joys of the heavenly country the soul of this stranger, who is the first that hath died among us in this island. But I beseech thee not to reveal the holy secret to any one during my life.'

Chapter Seven - Of a Vision of Angels Who Were Conducting the Soul of One Diormit to Heaven, Revealed to the Same Holy Man

AT another time, a certain Irish stranger came to the Saint, and abode with him for some months in the Iouan island (Iona). One day the blessed man says to him, 'Now is one of the clergy of thy province, whose name I do not yet know, being carried to heaven by angels.' But the brother, on hearing this, began to search within himself about the province of the Anteriores (East-erns), who in Scotic (Irish) are named Indairthir (men of East Oriel, in Ul-ster), and about the name of that blessed man; and then made this remark, saying, 'I know another soldier of Christ, named Diormit, who built for him-self a small monastery in the same district wherein I also was living.' The Saint says to him, 'He it is of whom thou art speaking, who has now been conducted into Paradise by the angels of God.'

But this also must very carefully be noted, that there were many secrets, holy mysteries, revealed to him by God, but concealed from others, which the same venerable man in no wise suffered to be brought to the knowledge of men; there being two reasons for this, as he himself once hinted to a few brethren, namely, that he might avoid vainglory, and, that he might not en-courage, for the purpose of asking questions of himself, intolerable crowds of persons wishing to make inquiries concerning him, when the fame of his rev-elations was spread abroad.

Chapter Eight - Of a Mighty Conflict of Angels against Demons, and of their Seasonably Assisting the Saint in the Same Combat

ANOTHER day the holy man, while living in the Iouan island (Iona), sought among the bushes a place more remote from men, and fit for prayer; and there, when he began to pray, on a sudden, as he himself afterwards told a few of the brethren, he sees over against him a very black host of demons fighting with iron darts, who, as had been revealed to the holy man by the Spirit, wished to invade his monastery, and to kill many of the brethren with the same weapons. But he, one man alone against innumerable foes such as they were, took the armour of the apostle Paul, and fought in hard conflict. And so for the greater part of the day was, the fighting continued on both sides, neither were they, though innumerable, able to conquer him, though but one; nor was he alone strong enough to drive them from his island, until the angels of God, as the Saint afterwards related to some few persons, came to his aid; and for fear of these the demons were terror-stricken and gave way. On the same day the Saint, on his return to the monastery after the put-ting to flight of the demons from his island, speaks this word about the same hostile bands, saying, 'Those deadly foes who on this day, by the mercy of God and the angels helping us, have been driven out from the bounds of this little land unto the Ethican land (Tiree), will there as savage invaders enter the monasteries of the brethren, and will bring in pestilential diseases, of which many, attacked by the sickness, will die.' Which so came to pass in those days, according to the foreknowledge of the blessed man. And after-wards, two days having intervened, the Spirit revealing it to him, he says, 'Baithene, by God's help, has managed that the congregation of the church over which by Divine Providence he presides, in the Plain of Lunge (in Tiree), is defended by fastings and prayers from the invasion of demons, where no one, except one who is already dead, will die this time.' Which was so fulfilled, according to his prophecy. For, while many in the other monasteries of the same island died of that disease, no one, except the one of whom the Saint spoke, died with Baithene, in his congregation.

Chapter Nine - Of an Apparition of Angels whom the Man of God Saw Carrying to Heaven the Soul of a Certain Blacksmith, Named Columb, Surnamed Coilrigin

A CERTAIN blacksmith was living in the central portion of Scotia (Ireland), very intent on almsdeeds, and abounding in other acts of righteousness. When this Columb above mentioned, surnamed Coilrigin, was come to his latter end in a good old age, in the same hour in which he was led forth from the body, St. Columba, then living in the Iouan island (Iona), thus spoke to some few seniors who were standing around: 'Columb Coilrigin,' he says, 'the blacksmith, has not laboured in vain; for out of the labour of his own hands has he, a happy purchaser, obtained eternal rewards. For, behold! now is his soul carried by holy angels to the joys of the heavenly country. For whatever he was able to acquire by the business of his craft, he spent upon alms for the poor.'

Chapter Ten - Of a Similar Vision of Angels Whom the Blessed Man Beheld Carrying To Heaven the Soul of a Certain Woman of Holy Life

IN like manner, at another time, the holy man, while living in the Iouan island (Iona), one day, suddenly raising his eyes to heaven, spoke these words: 'Happy woman, happy for thy holy life, whose soul even now the angels of God are carrying to Paradise!' Now there was a certain religious brother, Genere by name, a Saxon (Englishman) and a baker, engaged in baker's work, who had heard this word proceeding from the mouth of the Saint. And on the same day of the month, at the end of that year, the Saint says to the same Genere the Saxon, 'I see a wonderful thing. Behold! the woman of whom I spoke in thy presence a year ago is now meeting in the air the soul of a certain countryman, her husband, and, together with holy angels, is fighting for that soul against hostile powers; by their assistance, and the righteousness of the same poor man recommending him, his soul is snatched from the contentions of demons, and led through to the place of eternal refreshment.'

Chapter Eleven - Of An Apparition of Holy Angels whom St. Columba Saw Meeting on its Way the Soul of Blessed Brendan, the Founder of That Monastery Which in Scotic (Irish) is Named Birra (of Birr)

ANOTHER day in like manner, while the venerable man was living in the Iouan island (Iona), early in the morning he calls to him his oft-mentioned attendant, Diormit by name, and gives him directions, saying, 'Let the sacred ministrations of the Eucharist be quickly prepared. For to-day is the birthday (festival) of blessed Brendan.' 'Wherefore,' says the attendant, 'dost thou direct that such solemnities of masses be prepared on this day, for no messenger of the death of that holy man has come to us from Scotia (Ireland)?' 'Go,' then says the Saint, 'thou oughtest to obey my direction. For this last night I saw the heaven suddenly opened, and choirs of angels descending to meet the soul of the holy Brendan; by whose luminous and incomparable brightness the whole compass of the world was enlightened in that hour.'

Chapter Twelve - Of a Vision of Holy Angels who carried Up to Heaven the Soul of St. Columban Moculoigse, the Bishop

ON a certain day in like manner, while the brethren were putting on their shoes, and were preparing in the morning to go to the different occupations of the monastery, the Saint directs that on the contrary they keep holiday on that day, that the requisites for the sacred oblation be prepared, and that some addition be made to their frugal meal, as on the Lord's day. 'And me,' he says, 'however unworthy I may be, it behooves to celebrate the sacred mysteries of the Eucharist, out of veneration for that soul which this last night has been borne away amid the holy choirs of angels, and has ascended to Paradise beyond the starry tracts of the heavens.' Then the brethren obey these words, and, according to the bidding of the Saint, keep holiday that same day, and, the sacred ministries being prepared, they proceed to the church with the Saint, all arrayed in white, as on a solemn day. But it so happened that while among other such offices was sung with musical intonation that accustomed prayer in which the name of St. Martin is commemorated, the Saint, suddenly turning to the singers when they came to the place where his name occurs, says, 'To-day ye ought to sing for St. Columban the bishop.' Then all the brethren who were present understood that Columban, a bishop in Leinster and a dear friend of Columba, had passed away to the Lord. And after the space of some time, some persons coming from the province of Leinster announce that the same bishop had died during that night in which it was so revealed to the Saint.

Chapter Thirteen - Of an Apparition of Angels who came Down to Meet the Souls of Monks of St. Comgell

AT another time the venerable man, while living in the Iouan island (Iona), incited by some sudden impulse, rang his bell; and, when the brethren are assembled, he says, 'Now let us help by prayer the monks of the abbot Comgell, who are in this hour drowned in the Lough of the Calf (Belfast Lough); for, behold, at this moment they are warring in the air against hostile powers who are trying to snatch away the soul of a certain guest who is drowned along with them.' Then, after tearful and earnest prayer, he quickly rises before the altar with a joyful countenance, among the brethren who are at the same time prostrate in prayer, and says, 'Give thanks to Christ. For holy angels meeting holy souls have now delivered, as conquering warriors, even that guest also, snatched from the conflicts of warring demons.'

Chapter Fourteen - Of a Manifestation of Angels Meeting the Soul of One Emchath

AT another time the holy man, making his way beyond the Ridge of Britain (Drum-Alban) near the lake of the river Nisa (Loch Ness), being suddenly inspired by the Holy Spirit, says to the brethren who are journeying with him at that time, 'Let us make haste to meet the holy angels who, that they may carry away the soul of a certain heathen man, who is keeping the moral law of nature even to extreme old age, have been sent out from the highest regions of heaven, and are waiting until we come thither, that we may baptize him in time before he dies.' And, thus speaking, the aged Saint made as much haste as he could to go in advance of his companions, until he came to the district which is named Airchart-dan (Glen Urquhart). And a certain old man there found, Emchath by name, hearing the word of God preached by the Saint, and believing, was baptized, and immediately, joyful and safe, with the angels who were meeting him, passed away to the Lord. But his son Virolec also believed, together with his whole house, and was baptized.

Chapter Fifteen - Of the Angel of the Lord who at the Nick of Time So Quickly Helped a Certain Brother who had fallen from the Top of the Round Monastery in Durrow

AT another time, while the holy man was sitting writing in his little cell, suddenly his countenance is changed, and he pours forth this cry from his pure breast, saying, 'Help! Help!' But two brethren standing at the door, namely Colgu son of Cellach, and Lugne Mocublai, ask him the reason of such a sudden cry. To whom the venerable man gave this answer, saying, 'I have directed the angel of the Lord, who was just now standing among you, with all haste to help one of the brethren who has fallen from the top of the roof of the great house which is at the present time being built in the Plain of the Oakwood' (Durrow). And then the Saint added these words, saying, 'How wonderful and almost unspeakable is the swiftness of angelic flight, equal, as I think, to the rapidity of lightning. For that heavenly spirit who just now flew away from us hence, when that man began to slip, came to his help as it were in the twinkling of an eye, and bore him up before he could touch the ground; nor could he who fell perceive any fracture or injury. How amazing, I say, is this most rapid and seasonable help, which, quicker than can be said, with such great spaces of sea and land lying between, can so very rapidly be rendered.'

Chapter Sixteen - Of a Multitude of Holy Angels Seen Descending From Heaven for a Conference with the Blessed Man

AT another time again, the blessed man one day, while living in the Iouan island (Iona), the brethren being gathered together, charged them with great earnestness, saying to them, 'Today I desire to go out alone into the western plain of our island; therefore let none of you follow me.' And on their professing obedience, he goes out alone, as he wished. But a certain brother, a crafty, prying fellow, slipping off another way, secretly ensconces himself in the top of a certain little hill which overlooks the same plain; desiring, you see, to find out the cause of that solitary expedition of the blessed man. And when the same spy, from the top of the hillock, beheld him standing on a certain little hill on that plain, praying with his hands spread out to heaven, and lifting up his eyes to heaven: wonderful to say, behold then suddenly a marvellous sight appeared, which the same above-mentioned man, as I think, not without the permission of God, saw even with bodily eyes, from his place on the nearer little hill; that the name of the Saint, and the honour due to him, might afterwards, though against his own will, be the more spread abroad among the people on account of this vision thus vouchsafed. For holy angels, citizens of the celestial country, flying to him with wonderful swiftness, and clothed in white robes, began to stand around the holy man as he prayed; and. after some conversation with the blessed man, that heavenly host, as if perceiving itself to be under observation, quickly sped back to the highest heavens. And the blessed man himself, after the angelic conference, on his return to the monastery, again gathers the brethren together, and with no ordinary chiding inquires which of them is guilty of transgression. And, when they then declare that they do not know, the offender, conscious of his inexcusable transgression, and not enduring further to conceal his fault, on bended knees, in the midst of the choir of the brethren, as a suppliant, begs pardon before the Saint. The Saint, leading him aside, charges him, with severe threatening, as he kneels before him, that to no man must he disclose anything, not even a little secret, concerning that angelic vision, during the life of the same blessed man. But after the departure of the holy man from the body, he related that apparition of the heavenly host to the brethren, with solemn attestation. Whence, even to this day, the place of that angelic conference attests the event that took place there by its own proper name, which in Latin can be rendered Colliculus Angelorum; but in Scotic (Irish) Cnoc Angel (the Angels' hill, now Sithean Mor, the greater Fairies' hill). Wherefore we must direct our thoughts, and very carefully examine, how great and of what nature were those sweet visits of angels to the blessed man, for the most part in winter nights, as he was watching and praying in the more secret places, while others slept; visits which could in no way come to the knowledge of men, and no doubt were very numerous. And even if some of them could in any way be found out by men, whether by day or by night, these without a doubt were very few in comparison with those angelic visits which, mark you, could be known by no one. This also is in like manner to be noted concerning some luminous manifestations, which were found out by a few persons, and will be described below.

Chapter Seventeen - Of a Luminous Column Seen To Rise Flaming From the Head of the Holy Man

AT another time four holy founders of monasteries, coming over from Scotia (Ireland) to visit St. Columba, found him in Hinba island (Eilean-na-Naoimh, one of the Garveloch isles?); the names of which illustrious men were Comgell Mocu Aridi, Cainnech Mocu Dalon, Brendan Mocu Alti, and Cormac Ua Liathain. These all with one consent chose that St. Columba should consecrate before them in the church the sacred mysteries of the Eucharist. So he, complying with their bidding, on the Lord's day, according to custom, after the reading of the Gospel, enters the church together with them; and there, while the solemnities of masses were being celebrated, St. Brendan Mocu Alti saw, as he afterwards told Comgell and Cainnech, a certain globe of fire with a hairy tail, very luminous, rising upward, like some column, from the top of the head of St. Columba, as he was standing before the altar consecrating the holy oblation, and flaming, until such time as the same all-holy ministrations were completed.

Chapter Eighteen - Of the Descent or Visitation of the Holy Spirit, which in the Same Island for Three Days in Succession, and as Many Nights, Continued Over the Venerable Man

AT another time, while the holy man was sojourning in Hinba island (see chap, xvii), the grace of holy inspiration was poured out upon him in an abundant and incomparable manner, and wonderfully continued with him for three days; so that, for three days and as many nights, he remained within a house which was locked up and filled with celestial light, would suffer no man to come near him, and neither did eat nor drink. And from this house, mark you, rays of intense brightness were seen at night, breaking out through the chinks of the doors and the keyholes. Some spiritual songs also, which had not been heard before, were then heard as they were being sung by him. But he himself also, as he afterwards declared before a very few persons, saw, openly manifested, many secret things, hidden ever since the foundation of the world. Some obscure and most difficult passages of the sacred Scriptures appeared plain; and in that light were more clearly manifested to the eyes of his most pure heart. He lamented that Baithene his foster-son was not present; had he chanced to be there in those three days, he might have written down many things from the lips of the blessed man; mysteries unknown by other men, either concerning past ages, or those which were next to follow; and also some explanations of the sacred volumes. Baithene however could not be present, being detained by contrary winds in the Egean island (Eigg) until those three days and as many nights of that incomparable and glorious visitation came to a close.

Chapter Nineteen - Of the Angelical Brightness of the Light Which Virgno (Fergna), a Youth of Good Disposition, who Afterwards, By the Providence of God, Presided over This Church, Which I, Though Unworthy, Now Serve, Saw Descending over St. Columba in the Church, while the Brethren were Resting in their Beds One Winter's Night

ONE winter's night the above-mentioned Virgno, burning with the love of God, enters the church alone for the sake of prayer, while others were asleep, and there prayed devoutly in a certain side-house which abutted on the wall of the oratory. And after some considerable interval, say of about one hour, the venerable man Columba enters the same holy house, and, together with him, a golden light, descending from the utmost height of heaven, filling all that space of the church. But the brightness of the same celestial light, breaking through the inner door of that chamber, which was slightly open, filled the separate interior of that little side-house where Virgno was trying all he could to conceal himself, and not without some terrible fear. And as no summer and noonday sun can be gazed upon with direct and undazzled eyes, so also Virgno himself could in no wise bear the celestial brightness which he saw, because that incomparable flood of light completely dazzled the sight of his eyes. At the vision of this fearful splendour, as of the lightning's flash, the above-mentioned brother was terrified to that degree that there was no strength left in him. But St. Columba, after a short prayer, goes out of the church. And on the morrow he calls to him Virgno, who is greatly awe-stricken, and addresses him in these short consolatory words, saying, again and again, 'O my child, thou hast been very pleasing in the sight of God during the past night, casting thine eyes down to the ground, terrified by the fear of His brightness; for, if thou hadst not so done, thine eyes would have been blinded at the sight of that inestimable light. But this must thou carefully observe; never to disclose to any one during my life so rare a manifestation of light.' And so this famous and wonderful occurrence became known to many after the departure of the same blessed man, from the narration of the same Virgno. Indeed, Comman, an honourable presbyter, sister's son to the same Virgno, gave an account to me, Adamnan, about the above vision, written out at some time or other, and duly witnessed. And he also had heard it related by the lips of the abbot Virgno himself, his uncle, who, as far as he could, had seen that vision.

Chapter Twenty - Of another Almost Similar Vision of Great Brightness

ANOTHER night also, one of the brethren, Colga by name, son of Aedh Draigniche, of the race of Fechureg, of whom we made mention in the first book (Ch. 17); came by chance to the door of the church while others were sleeping, and there stood for some time and prayed. Then in the next place he sees the whole church filled with celestial light: which light indeed, quicker than can be said, vanished like lightning from his gaze. But he was not aware that St. Columba was at that hour praying within the church. And after such a sudden apparition of light he returns home in great alarm. On the next day the Saint, calling him to him, rebuked him sharply, saying, 'Take care from this time, my son, that thou dost not, like a prying person, endeavour to search into that heavenly light which has not been granted to thee, because it will flee from thee; and do not tell any one, in my days, what thou hast seen.'

Chapter Twenty-One - Of another Corresponding Apparition of Divine Light

AT another time again, to a certain foster-son of his in pursuit of learning, of the name of Berchan, whose surname was Mesloen, the blessed man one day gave strict orders, saying, 'Take care, my son, that to-night thou approach not my little dwelling, as thou art always wont to do.' After hearing this, notwithstanding the prohibition, he went to the house of the blessed man in the silence of night, while others were sleeping, and, slyly prying, put his eyes straight to the keyholes, evidently thinking that, as the event proved, some celestial vision would be manifested to the Saint within. For, in the same hour, that little dwelling of the blessed man was filled with the splendour of celestial brightness, which that young transgressor could not bear to look upon; and so he fled from the place. The Saint on the morrow, leading him aside, and rebuking him with great severity, addresses him in these words; saying, 'This last night, my son, thou hast sinned before God; for thou didst foolishly imagine that the prying of thy secret artfulness could be concealed, or hidden from the Holy Spirit. Did not I see thee coming to the door of my little dwelling in that hour, and thence returning? And if I had not at the same moment prayed for thee, thou mightest there, before the door, either have fallen down dead, or thine eyes might have been plucked out of their sockets. But the Lord hath spared thee this time for my sake. And know this, that while living in luxury in thine Irish fatherland, thy face shall burn with shame all the days of thy life. But this I have obtained from the Lord in prayer, that because thou art my foster-child, thou shalt do a tearful penance before thy death, and obtain mercy from God.' All which things, according to the word of the blessed man, so happened to him afterwards, as they had been prophesied concerning him.

Chapter Twenty-Two - Of another Apparition of Angels Manifested to the Holy Man, those, Namely, whom He Saw Setting Out to Meet His Holy Soul, When it was as if Soon About to Depart from the Body

AT another time, while the blessed man was living in the Iouan island (Iona), one day his holy face lighted up with a certain wondrous and joyous cheerfulness, and, lifting up his eyes to heaven, filled with incomparable joy, he was intensely gladdened. Then, after a moderate interval of some little moment or so, that savoury and delightful gladness is turned into a mournful sadness. Now the two men who at that hour were standing at the door of his little cell, which was constructed on a higher spot, being also themselves greatly saddened together with him, of whom the one was Lugne Mocublai, but the other was named Pilu, a Saxon (Englishman), inquire the cause of that sudden gladness, and of that subsequent sadness. To whom the Saint thus speaks: 'Go in peace, and do not now ask of me that the cause of that gladness or even of the sadness be manifested to you.' On hearing this, all in tears, and kneeling down with faces prostrate on the ground, they beseech him with supplication, desiring to know something of that thing which had

been revealed to the Saint in the same hour. And, seeing them greatly saddened, he says, 'Because I love you, I will not give way to sadness. Ye must
promise jne first that never in my lifetime will ye betray to any man the holy
secret about which ye are inquiring.' And they at once, according to his in-
junction, readily promised. And, after such promise, the venerable man thus
speaks to them, saying, 'Up to this present day, thirty years of my sojourning
in Britain are accomplished. Meanwhile, for many days past I have devoutly
besought my Lord, that at the end of this present thirtieth year He would release me from my dwelling here, and call me thither to the celeetial country.
And this was the cause of my gladness, about which you in your sorrow are
asking me. For I saw holy angels sent from the throne on high to meet me,
and to lead out my soul from the flesh. But behold now, suddenly held back,
they are standing on a rock on the other side of the Sound of our island, evidently wishing to come near, to call me away from the body unto them. But
they are not permitted to come nearer, and are soon to speed their flight to
the highest heavens; because that which the Lord granted me, when I prayed
with all my might, that on this day I might pass away from the world to Himself, He, giving more heed to the prayers of many churches for me, hath
changed quicker than can be said. To which churches, indeed, so praying for
me, it has been granted by the Lord, that, although against mine own will,
four years from this day are added for my remaining in the flesh. This delay,
so sad for me, has not unreasonably been the cause of my sadness to-day.
And when, you see, these four years yet to come in this life, please God, are
ended, I shall pass away rejoicing to the Lord, by a sudden departure, without any previous bodily pain, with holy angels coming to meet me at that
time.' According to these words, which, as is said, the venerable man did not
speak without much sighing and sadness, and also great shedding of tears, he
remained in the flesh after that for four years.

Chapter Twenty-Three - Of the Passing Away to the Lord of Our Holy Patron Columba

SHORTLY before the end of the above-mentioned four years, after the fulfilment of which, as he, a true prophet, knew long beforehand, the term of his
present life was to be completed; one day in the month of May, as we have
written above in the second book (Ch. 27), the old man, borne in a wagon,
being feeble with age, goes to visit the working brethren. To whom, while at
their labours in the western part of the Iouan island (Iona), on that day he
began to speak thus; saying, 'During the Paschal solemnity in the month of
April last past, with desire I desired to pass away to Christ the Lord; as indeed had been granted me by Him, if I had preferred it. But, lest your festival
of gladness should be turned into sorrow, I chose rather that the day of my
departure out of the world should be put off a little longer.' The monks of his

household, when they heard from him these mournful tidings, were greatly distressed, and he began to cheer them, so far as in him lay, with words of consolation. Which being ended, as he was sitting in the carriage, he turned his face to the east, and blessed the island with the dwellers in that island home; from which day, as has been written in the above-mentioned book (Book Two, Ch. 28), the poisons of the three-cleft tongues of vipers even to this day have not been able in any way to hurt either man or beast. After those words of benediction the Saint is carried back to his monastery.

Then, in the next place, in the course of a few days, while the solemnities of masses were being celebrated, according to custom, on the Lord's day; all on a sudden the face of the venerable man, as his eyes are lifted upward, is seen suffused with a ruddy glow, for, as it is written, 'When the heart is glad the face blooms.' For in that same hour he alone saw an angel of the Lord hovering above within the walls of his oratory. And, because the lovely and tranquil aspect of the holy angels pours joy and gladness into the hearts of the elect, this was the cause of that sudden gladness imparted to the blessed man. And when those who were therein present inquired as to what, mark you, was the cause of the joy that was kindled within him, the Saint, looking upward, gave them this reply: 'Wonderful and incomparable is the subtilty of the nature of angels. For. behold, an angel of the Lord, sent to demand some deposit dear to God, looking down from above upon us within the church, and blessing us, has returned again through the vaulting of the church, and has left no traces of such an exit.' So far the Saint. But yet, as to the nature of that deposit for which the angel was sent to make inquiry, not one of those who were standing around was able to form an opinion Our patron, however, gave the name of a holy deposit to his own soul, which had been entrusted to him by God; which soul, as will be narrated below, in the night of the next Lord's day, six days in succession coming between, passed away to the Lord.

And so the venerable man at the end of the same week, that is on the Sabbath day (Saturday), himself and his dutiful attendant Diormit, go to bless the granary, which was close at hand. On entering which, when he blessed both it and two heaps of corn that were stored therein, he uttered these words with giving of thanks, saying, 'I greatly congratulate the monks of my household that this year also, if I should have to depart from you to any place, ye will have enough for the year.' On hearing this saying, Diormit his attendant began to be sorrowful, and to speak thus: 'In the course of this year, Father, thou art often making us sorrowful, because thou so frequently makest mention of thy departure.' To whom the Saint gave this reply, 'I have some little secret discourse, and if thou wilt faithfully promise me not to disclose it to any one before my death, I shall be able to give thee some clearer intimation concerning my departure.' When the attendant, on bended knees, had completed some such promise, according to the wish of the Saint, the venerable man in the next place thus speaks: 'This day is in the sacred volumes called Sabbath, which is, being interpreted, Rest. And for me this day is a Sabbath indeed, because it is the last day of this my present laborious life, in which I take my rest after all the wearinesses of my labours. And in the middle of this most solemn night (eve) of the Lord's day that is now coming, according to the saying of the Scriptures, "I shall go the way of my fathers." For even now my Lord Jesus Christ deigneth to invite me, to Whom, I say, in the middle of this night, I shall depart, at His invitation. For thus it hath been revealed unto me by the Lord Himself.' The attendant on hearing these sad words began to weep bitterly, but the Saint endeavoured to console him as well as he could.

After this, the Saint goes out of the granary, and, returning to the monastery, sits down at the half-way, in which place a cross, afterwards fixed in a millstone, and standing at this day, is to be seen on the side of the road. And while the Saint, feeble with age, as I said before, sat down for a little while and rested in that place, behold! there comes up to him the white horse, that faithful servant, mark you, that used to carry the milk-pails between the cow-pasture (or byre?) and the monastery. This creature then coming up to the Saint, wonderful to say, putting its head in his bosom, as I believe under the inspiration of God, in Whose sight every animal is endowed with a sense of things, because the Creator Himself hath so ordered it; knowing that his master would soon depart from him, and that he would see his face no more, began to utter plaintive moans, and, as if a man, to shed tears in abundance into the Saint's lap, and so to weep, frothing greatly. Which when the attendant saw, he began to drive away that weeping mourner; but the Saint forbad him, saying, 'Let him alone! As he loves me so, let him alone; that into this my bosom he may pour out the tears of his most bitter lamentation. Behold! thou, even seeing that thou art a man, and hast a rational soul, couldest in no way know anything about my departure, except what I myself have lately shown to thee; but to this brute animal, destitute of reason, in what way soever the Maker Himself hath willed, He hath revealed that his master is about to go away from him.' And, so saying, he blessed his sorrowing servant the horse, then turning about to go away from him.

And going forth thence, he ascended the little hill that overlooks the monastery, and stood for a little while on the top of it, and, standing with both hands lifted up, he blessed the monastery, saying, 'To this place, small and mean though it be, not only the Scotic kings (Irish and Dalriadic) with their peoples, but also the rulers of strange and foreign nations, with the people subject to them, shall bring great and extraordinary honour; by the Saints also of other churches shall no common reverence be shown.'

After these words, descending from that little hill, and returning to the monastery, he sat in his cell transcribing the Psalter; and coming to that verse of the thirty-third (34th) Psalm where it is written, 'But they who seek the Lord shall want no manner of thing that is good,' 'Here,' he says, 'at the end of the page, I must cease. What follows let Baithene write.' The last verse which he had written was very suitable for the Saint at his departure, to whom eternal things that are good shall never be wanting; while the following verse was most suitable for his successor, as a father and teacher of spiritual sons: 'Come, ye children, and hearken unto me; I will teach you the fear of the Lord.' And indeed he, as his predecessor enjoined, succeeded him not only in teaching, but also in transcribing.

After the transcription of the aforesaid verse, at the end of the page, the Saint enters the church for the evening mass (evensong) of the Lord's day night (eve), and as soon as this is over he returns to his cell, where he had bare rock for his bedding, and a stone for his pillow, which at this day is standing by his grave as a kind of sepulchral monument; and he sits on the bed through the night. And so, there sitting, he gives his last commands to the brethren, in the hearing of his attendant only; saying, 'These last words, O my children, I commend unto you; that ye have mutual and unfeigned charity among yourselves, with peace. And if, according to the example of the holy fathers, ye shall attend to this, God, the Comforter of good men, will help you; and I, abiding with Him, will intercede for you. And not only shall the necessaries of this present life be sufficiently supplied by Him, but He will also bestow those rewards of eternal riches, which are laid up for them that keep His Divine laws.' Thus far we have drawn up, recounted in a short paragraph, the last words of our venerable patron, spoken just as he was passing over from this weary pilgrimage unto the heavenly country.

After which, as his happy last hour gradually approached, the Saint was silent. Then, in the next place, in the middle of the night, at the sound of the ringing of the bell, he rises in haste and goes to the church; and, running more quickly than the rest, he enters alone, and on bended knees falls down in prayer beside the altar. Diormit his attendant, following more slowly, at the same moment sees from a distance that the whole church is filled within, in the direction of the Saint, with angelic light. But when he approaches the door, the same light that he had seen, which was also seen by a few other of the brethren, as they were standing at a distance, quickly disappeared. So Diormit, entering the church, keeps on asking, in a lamentable voice, 'Where art thou, Father?' And, feeling his way through the darkness, the lights of the brethren not yet being brought in, he finds the Saint prostrate before the altar; and, lifting him up a little and sitting beside him, he placed the holy head in his bosom. And meanwhile, the congregation of monks running up with the lights, and seeing their father dying, began to weep. And, as we have learnt from some who were there present, the Saint, his soul not yet departing, with his eyes opened upward, looked about on either hand with a wonderful cheerfulness and joy of countenance; doubtless seeing the holy angels coming to meet him. Then Diormit lifts up the holy right hand of the Saint that he may bless the choir of monks. But also the venerable man himself, so far as he could, at the same time moved his hand, so that, mark you, he might still be seen, while passing away, to bless the brethren by the motion of his hand, though he was not able to do so with his voice. And, after his holy benediction thus expressed, he immediately breathed out his spirit. Which having left the tabernacle of the body, his face remained ruddy, and wonderfully gladdened by an angelic vision; so that it appeared not to be that of one dead, but of one living and sleeping. Meanwhile the whole church resounded with mournful lamentations.

But there is a thing which seems not one to be passed over, which was revealed to a certain Saint of Ireland at the same hour in which his blessed soul departed. For in that monastery which in the Scotic (Irish) tongue is named Cloni-finchoil (Rosnarea?) there was a certain holy man, an aged soldier of Christ, just and wise, who was named Lugud son of Tailchan. Now this man early in the morning, with many sighs, related his vision to one who was, equally with himself, a Christian soldier, Fergno by name; saying, 'In the middle of this last night, the holy Columba, the pillar of many churches, passed away to the Lord. And in the hour of his blessed departure, I saw in the spirit the whole of the Iouan island (Iona), to which I have never come in the body, irradiated by the brightness of angels, and the whole space of the air up to the ethereal regions of the heavens illumined by the brightness of the same angels, who, sent from heaven, descended in countless numbers to bear away his holy soul. High-sounding strains also, and very sweet songs of the angelic hosts, did I hear in the very moment of the departure of his holy soul among the angelic choirs ascending up on high.' Virgno (Fergno), rowing over in those days from Scotia (Ireland), and spending the remaining days of his life in Hinba island (Eilean-na-Naoimh, one of the Garveloch isles?), used very often to narrate to the monks of St. Columba this vision of angels. And he, as has been said above, had undoubtedly heard it from the lips of that aged Saint to whom it had been revealed. Which Virgno, to wit, after many years completed among the brethren in obedience and without reproach, completed other twelve years in a place of anchorites in Muirbulcmar (in Hinba?), leading an anchorite's life, a victorious soldier of Christ. This aforesaid vision we have not only found committed to writing, but have heard related without any hesitation by some experienced elders to whom Virgno himself had related it.

Another vision also, revealed at the same hour in a different way, one of those who saw it, a soldier of Christ, a very old man, whose name also can be expressed as Ferreolus, but in Scotic (Irish) Ernene (diminutive of Iarn. iron), of the clan Mocufirroide, who among the remains of other monks of St. Columba, himself also a holy monk, buried in the Ridge of Tomma (Drumhome), is waiting for the resurrection with the Saints, he, I say, related it to me, Adamnan, a youth at that time, with most assured testimony, saying, 'In that night in which St. Columba, by a happy and blessed death, passed away from earth to heaven, I and other men with me, while labouring in the taking of fish in the valley of the fishful river Fenda (the Finn, co. Donegal), saw the whole space of the aerial sky suddenly illuminated. Struck by the suddenness of this miracle, we lifted up our eyes and turned them to the east, and, lo! there appeared as it were some very great fiery pillar, which as it ascended upward in the middle of that night appeared to us to enlighten the whole world, even as the summer's noonday sun. And after that pillar had ascended through the sky, then darkness followed, as after the setting of the sun. And so not only did we, who were together in that place, behold with vast admiration the brightness of this luminous and remarkable pillar; but many other fishermen also, who were fishing here and there about the different river fishpools of the same river, were struck by a great fear at the sight of a like apparition, as they afterwards related to us.' The miracles, then, of these three visions appearing in that same hour of the departure of our venerable patron, bear witness to the eternal honours conferred upon him by the Lord. Let us now return to our main subject.

Meanwhile, after the departure of his holy soul, the hymns for the morning being ended, the sacred body is carried back, with the tuneful psalmody of the brethren, from the church to the cell from which a little before he had come alive. And for three days and as many nights his august obsequies are celebrated with all due honour and ceremonial. And these being ended in the sweet praises of God, the venerable body of our holy and blessed patron, wrapped in clean linen cloths and placed in a coffin (or grave?) that was prepared for it, is buried with due reverence, to rise again in luminous and eternal brightness.

Now, what has been told us by experienced men concerning those above-mentioned three days of the obsequies, accomplished in due ecclesiastical form, shall here be narrated, towards the close of this book. For, indeed, on one occasion a certain one of the brethren, speaking in a simple way in the presence of the venerable man, says to the Saint, 'After thy death, all the people of these provinces will row across to celebrate thine obsequies, and will fill this Iouan island (Iona).' On hearing this saying, the Saint immediately replies, 'my child, the event will not prove to be as thou sayest, for a promiscuous throng of the common people will in no wise be able to come to my obsequies. The monks of my household alone will execute my burial rites, and honour the funeral offices.' Which prophetic saying of his the omnipotence of God caused to be fulfilled immediately after his departure; for, during those three days and nights of the obsequies, there came a great storm of wind without rain, which being an effectual obstacle, no one carried in a small boat was able to cross the Sound in either direction. And after the completion of the burial of the blessed man, the storm was stayed, and the wind ceased, and the whole of the sea became calm.

Let the reader therefore weigh well in how great and in what manner of honour our famous patron is esteemed in the sight of God, to whom at one time and another, while he was living in mortal flesh, God granted that at his prayer storms were stayed and seas made calm. And again, when he found it necessary, on the above-mentioned occasion, the gales of winds arose when he wished, and the stormy seas were lashed into fury. And then immediately, as has been said above, when the rites of his burial were completed, they were turned into a great calm.

This, then, was the end of our illustrious patron's life, those, the beginnings of his deserts, who, according to passages of the Scriptures, is a sharer in eternal triumphs, added to the Fathers, united with the Apostles and Prophets, gathered in the number of the white-robed thousands of the Saints who have washed their robes in the blood of the Lamb; he followeth the Lamb as his leader, a virgin immaculate, pure from every stain, through the grace of our Lord Jesus Christ Himself; to Whom with the Father is ascribed honour, virtue, praise, glory, and eternal dominion, in the unity of the Holy Spirit, for ever and ever.

After reading these three little books, let each diligent reader note well of how great and of what manner of merit was our holy and venerable abbot, so often mentioned above; of how great and of what manner of honour he was esteemed in the sight of God; how great and on what manner were those angelical and luminous visits to himself; how great was the grace of prophecy that was in him; how great the efficacy of Divine virtues; how great and how frequent the brightness of Divine light that shone around him while yet abiding in this mortal flesh; which same celestial brightness, even after the departure of his most kindly soul from the tabernacle of the body, does not cease to shine around the place in which his sacred bones rest; where also there is a frequent visitation of angels, as is considered proved, being shown to certain chosen persons. And this extraordinary favour has also been conferred by God on the same man of blessed memory, by which, though he lived in this small and remote island of the British sea, his name has merited to be honourably noised abroad, not only throughout the whole of our own Scotia (Ireland), and Britain, the greatest of all the islands of the whole world; but to reach even as far as three-cornered Spain, and the Gauls, and Italy, which lies beyond the Pennine Alps, yea, even to the city of Rome itself, which is the head of all cities. So great and such notable honour is known, among other marks of Divine favour, to have been conferred on the same Saint by God, Who loves them that love Him, and, more and more glorifying those who magnify Him with sweet praises, lifts them up on high with immeasurable honours, Who is blessed for ever. Amen.

I beseech those, whoever they may be, that wish to transcribe these books, yea rather, I adjure them by Christ the Judge of the worlds, that after they have diligently transcribed, they will collate and correct them with all care, according to the copy from which they have written, and also subscribe this adjuration in its place:-

Whosoever reads these books of the virtues of Columba, let him pray God for me, Dorbhene, that I may possess eternal life after death.